T0309917

# Herman Melville's Ship of State

## Other Books of Interest from St. Augustine's Press

James V. Schall, *On the Principles of Taxing Beer:*
*And Other Brief Philosophical Essays*

James V. Schall, *At a Breezy Time of Day*

Promise Hsu, *China's Quest for Liberty: A Personal History of Freedom*

Marvin R. O'Connell, *Telling Stories that Matter: Memoirs and Essays*

Rémi Brague, *Moderately Modern*

Josef Pieper, *Exercises in the Elements: Essays–Speeches–Notes*

Josef Pieper, *A Journey to Point Omega: Autobiography from 1964*

Peter Kreeft, *Socrates' Children: The 100 Greatest Philosophers*

Peter Kreeft, *Ethics for Beginners: 52 "Big Ideas" from 32 Great Minds*

John von Heyking, *Comprehensive Judgment and Absolute Selflessness:*
*Winston Churchill on Politics as Friendship*

Joseph Bottum, *The Decline of the Novel*

D. Q. McInerny, *Being Ethical*

Roger Scruton, *An Intelligent Person's Guide to Modern Culture*

Roger Scruton, *The Meaning of Conservatism: Revised 3rd Edition*

Roger Scruton, *The Politics of Culture and Other Essays*

Roger Scruton, *On Hunting*

Leon J. Podles, *Losing the Good Portion:*
*Why Men Are Alienated from Christianity*

Allen Mendenhall, *Shouting Softly: Lines on Law, Literature, and Culture*

René Girard, *A Theater of Envy: William Shakespeare*

Marion Montgomery, *With Walker Percy at the Tupperware Party*

Charles R. Embry and Glenn Hughes, editors, *The Timelessness of Proust:*
*Reflections on In Search of Lost Time*

Frederic Raphael and Joseph Epstein, *Where Were We?:*
*The Conversation Continues*

C. S. Lewis and Don Giovanni Calabria, *The Latin Letters of C. S. Lewis*

# Herman Melville's
# Ship of State

## WILL MORRISEY

ST. AUGUSTINE'S PRESS
South Bend, Indiana

Manufactured in the United States of America.

1  2  3  4  5  6   26  25  24  23  22  21  20

**Library of Congress Control Number: 2020941898**


∞ The paper used in this publication meets the minimum requirements of the American National Standard for Information Sciences – Permanence of Paper for Printed Materials, ANSI Z39.48-1984.

St. Augustine's Press
www.staugustine.net

# Table of Contents

# INTRODUCTION:
# THE DEMOCRATIC DILEMMA

In 1840, Alexis de Tocqueville published the second volume of *Democracy in America*, his magisterial study based on observations he had made on his nine-month visit to the United States nearly a decade earlier. Although we Americans understandably read his book as a treatise about ourselves, Tocqueville wanted less to understand America than to understand democracy. By "democracy" he meant not primarily a political regime of the kind seen in ancient Athens or in a modern-day New England township, but the condition of social equality, a society free of an aristocratic class legally entitled to rule 'the commoners.' In America, everyone is a commoner, and those who pretend otherwise invite ridicule. As an aristocrat himself, Tocqueville saw the decline of his class in Europe, a decline accelerated by both monarchy and republicanism in his own country. He called America "the sample democracy" in the world, the place to go to see what an egalitarian society looked like, how it thought and felt, its "habits of the mind and heart"— habits soon coming to a country near you, my fellow noblemen.

What political regimes would such societies see? Without the possibility of the rule of 'the few,' that left the rule of 'the one' or 'the many.' And because the long-ago replacement of small, ancient city-states with large modern nation-states precluded the direct rule of the people, rule of the many in the modern rule would mean representative government, republicanism. The regime alternatives for democratic societies in modern states were republicanism and despotism—to be seen, Tocqueville remarks, in America and Russia, respectively, "each destined to hold half the world in its hands one day." To outline the structure of his preferred republican regime, he simply wrote an able summary of *The Federalist*, whose institutional structures might be adapted, although not simply carried over, by other 'founders' of republican regimes in other countries. But to describe democracy's habits of heart and mind, the subtle and not-so-subtle ways in which egalitarian social conditions pervade the souls of those who live amidst them, this took several hundred pages.

The 1840s also saw the return to America of another voyager, Herman Melville. At the time Tocqueville was bringing out his Volume II, the young American, ten years Tocqueville's junior, was signing up for his first whaling adventure, which began at the beginning of 1841. For nearly four years Melville experienced the democratic despotism of life at sea under several captains on a variety of ships, intermingled with sojourns on islands in the South Pacific, where a life of hedonist freedom rested uneasily on binges of cannibalism. The young sailor enjoyed the freedom without partaking of the fare; worrying that one day he might become part of a feast, he cut his island idyll short. For him, the remedy for shipboard despotism was either rebellion (he joined one mutiny) or exile (his adventures on shore occurred after he jumped his first ship).

The America he returned to in October 1944 was about to elect James K. Polk to the presidency. Along with Senator Stephen Douglas of Illinois and former president Franklin Pierce, Polk was part of a new intellectual and political movement which registered a generational shift in the American conception of the right basis for law and liberty. Whereas the founding generation had understood republican regime-building as an attempt to secure unalienable natural rights for "all men" under that regime, and the generation after that was divided over whether "all men" included slaves (New England said yes, the South, increasingly, said no), this third generation of Americans began to see republicanism less as security for rights as security for, and the best expression of, democracy itself, of the social egalitarianism Tocqueville had described. Might that not lead to majority tyranny, the rule of 'the people' in its might instead of popular sovereignty under the laws of nature and of nature's God?

Having just voyaged on seas even broader than the American continent, seas where might is indeed taken to make right, whether in the form of a captain on a ship or of mighty Leviathan underneath that ship, Melville had seen that a diverse and egalitarian society could find its ruler not in a popular majority but in one person. With no aristocratic class to serve as mediator between the one and the many, each pole of the political world would threaten the other. Fear of the many might cause the one to rule by fear absolutized, by terror. Tocqueville never wrote on Napoleon or on the Russian czar. In *Moby-Dick*, Melville did.

He could do so because he had survived and learned from what might be described as the photographic negative of Tocqueville's experience: Instead of voyaging to democratic-republican America from a Europe beset by unstable monarchies, a declining aristocracy, and constant threats of war and violent revolution, Melville had voyaged from America to societies in the condition of a state of nature—communitarian and pleasure-loving, to be sure, but with a sinister undercurrent of manslaughter, the faint smell of blood mingling with fragrance of the tropical flowers. He had voyaged on ships ruled by 'princes' (with the title of captain) wielding absolute power unknown to American landholders, even to the most adventurous pioneers. Returning to America, he too had an outsider's perspective, the ability to think like what we now call a political comparativist. In *Moby-Dick* he shows what a multi-ethnic, multi-religious democratic society would be under the regime of tyranny.

# CHAPTER ONE
# *MOBY-DICK* AND THE "YOUNG AMERICA"

On the frontispiece of his book, Melville quotes John Milton's *Paradise Lost*: "Leviathan, hugest of living creatures," embodies a double paradox: He "seems a moving land" and "his breath spouts out a sea." Land and water, breath and water: These are the terms of God's creation in Genesis. Turning immediately to the "etymology" of the word "whale," Melville quotes the English geographer, chaplain, and writer Richard Hakluyt, present at the genesis of the English settlement of North America as a promoter of the Jamestown colony; like Hakluyt, does Melville also intend to be a founder in the 'New World'? Hakluyt writes, "While you take in hand to school others, and teach them by what name a whale-fish is to be called in your own tongue, leaving out, through ignorance, the letter H, which almost alone maketh up the signification of the word, you deliver that which is not true" (781).[1]

Why so? The letter 'H' in Hebrew signifies "behold," referring to the way we hold our breath when gazing at (for example) the hugest of living creatures. God's prophets often tell His people to behold in awe the works of God. For His part, God gives life to the clay that becomes man by breathing into it. More still, according to learned rabbis the word *haishim* refers to the fiery inner core or fiery "souls" of the atoms that compose the world God created. Above all, the Tetragrammaton, which stands for God's unspeakable name, consists of the letters YHVH; further, *Hashem* means *the* Name. Melville's book will ask his readers to behold water, breath, and fire, along with a massive 'land' or mass of solid matter which moves like the earth in an earthquake, killing its would-be conquerors and sending them, as the old saying goes, to a watery grave. In the Book of Genesis, the

---

1   All page references to *Moby-Dick* are to Herman Melville: *Redburn, White-Jacket, Moby-Dick* (New York: Literary Classics of the United States, 1983).

Creator-God separates chaotic water from stable land. As a "moving land" with breath spouting water, Leviathan challenges or seems to challenge the principle of separation God follows throughout his act of creation—beginning with the separateness of Creator from created, but continuing to the separation of land from water and the differentiation of the many kinds of created things in His creation and even the differentiation of his human creations into male and female.

But the greatest challenge to God's authority in *Paradise Lost* comes from Milton's most famous character, Satan, whom the poet depicts as a sort of classical warrior-hero gone very wrong. Having rebelled against God, having been exiled or separated from God's Kindgom in Heaven, Satan attempts to ruin God's creation by provoking God to do what Satan himself lacks the power to do: bring death to the human ruler of the paradise within that creation. The Romantic philosophers and poets often admired Milton's Satan, one of them going so far as to say that Milton was on the devil's side without knowing it.

Whose side is Melville on? He confided to his friend Nathaniel Hawthorne that his book's secret motto was *Ego non baptisto te in nomine patris, sed in nomine diabolic*—an invocation his Captain Ahab pronounces while baptizing his harpoon with the blood of his three pagan harpooneers.[2] Melville could let Hawthorne in on the secret, having read Hawthorne's short story, "Young Goodman Brown," which culminates in the calamity of the protagonist's satanic baptism; Hawthorne, too, understood the dark side of human life better than their New England and New York City literary contemporaries. Yet Ahab loses his battle with the Whale, and only Ishmael survives to tell us of it. What does Ishmael want his readers to learn from his tale? What does Melville want them to learn? Both Ishmael and Melville have taught school, even as Hakluyt would teach teachers in his books; they are no strangers to the authority of teaching, with its precepts and commands.

2    In his brilliant account of Melville's thoughts on Shakespeare, Charles Olson pulls out a longer Latin tag Melville wrote on the fly-leaf of his copy of the volume containing the tragedies: *Ego non baptize te in nomine Patris et Filii et Spiritus Sancti—sed in nominee Diaboli.* As Olson notes, in the secret motto Melville disclosed to Hawthorne he retained the reference to God the Father but omitted the Son and the Holy Spirit. See Charles Olson: *Call Me Ishmael: A Study of Melville* (San Francisco: City Lights Books, 1947).

Melville next provides a list of eighty quotes or "extracts" from various authors ranging from Moses to Thomas Hobbes to Thomas Jefferson to Nantucket balladeers. The Hebrew Bible reveals that God created the whale and also will punish it with death; Hobbes calls the modern state, made by human "art," the "great Leviathan"—it is "an artificial man" who rules absolutely; Jefferson describes the Spermacetti Whale naturalistically, as "an active, fierce animal" which "requires vast address and boldness in he fishermen" who sail out of Nantucket to kill it; the whalers themselves combine Hobbes and Jefferson, singing of "the rare old Whale" as "a giant in might" of the ocean, "where might is right." The whale is natural, not artificial, but like Hobbes's Leviathan a king, "King of the boundless sea" (782–787). In Hobbes, the artificial mighty Leviathan, the modern state, imposes order on the chaos of the state of nature, composed of atoms; for the republican Jefferson, who most emphatically disbelieves that might makes right and that nature lacks moral laws, the men who hunt the whale are the heroes. Without saying so, Melville addresses the Jeffersonian founding of the United States of America, with its grounding in natural right, the laws of Nature and of Nature's God. He has in mind a new American Founding.

Melville titles his first chapter "Loomings," accustoming readers to his Shakespearean fondness for puns, and thereby his fondness for Shakespearean language and themes. "Loomings" means portents; dangers loom. "Loomings" also mean the weaved garments produced on looms, symbolic of Fate's work if not God's. Looms are for yarn; this sailor's yarn or story begins, famously, "Call me Ishmael" (795). That sentence does not declare, nor does it question, nor does it request; it commands. Ruling, and therefore politics, will loom large here.

Why choose "Ishmael" as the name one wants to be called, at the outset of the yarn? Genesis 16 relates events leading to the founding of Israel, God's covenant with Abram, thereafter Abraham or "father of many nations." The Flood, the return of chaotic water over all the land, wiped away the increasingly evil world of postlapsarian humanity; God set down the Noachide Commandments to govern all men. But the covenant with Abraham legislates for a particular regime, the regime for God's chosen people, a people commanded to do and to be better than the general run of nations. The problem is that Abraham's wife is sterile. She gives Abram her maid as a second wife, enabling him to generate a child and continue his people.

Hagar—another 'H' name—wants nothing to do with the plan, but an angel of God persuades her to consummate the marriage, promising that her son—to be named Ishmael, meaning, "The LORD has heard thy affliction"—will be the first of a multitude. More ominously, Ishmael "will be a wild man; his hand will be against every man, and every man's hand against him." His people will not be the children of the Covenant, the children of Abraham and Sarah born after God makes Sarah able to bear children despite her great age. At the same time, God promises that Ishmael will beget twelve princes as the progenitor of "a great nation."

The English settlers in New England regarded themselves as founders of regimes governed by the laws of the Covenant. They were spiritual descendants of Abraham through Israel, not through Ishmael. It should be noticed that the Jamestown settlement Hakluyt assisted in founding was not so governed; rather, it was a mercantile establishment. If not of Israel, then, necessarily of Ishmael. The United States of America, the American people, formed a tensile combination of Israelite and Ishmaelite characters. Melville's Ishmael journeys to New Bedford, Massachusetts on his way to Nantucket—an Ishmael in Israelite territory itself now partly given over to the commercial purposes of the whaling industry. To what extent can the awe-inspiring whale be merely an object of acquisition and trade? In finding out, this Ishmael will learn things Americans who stay on land do not know.

Melville had learned those things on his own whaling voyages in the early 1840s. He returned to an America whose intellectual and political classes saw a generational shift in political intentions. The "Young America" movement gathered such prominent political figures as presidents James K. Polk and Franklin Pierce and Illinois Senator Stephen Douglas. Following the call of the writer John L. O'Sullivan for America's "Manifest Destiny" to rule the remainder of the middle of the North American continent, Young America, while staying within the dominant Democratic Party, combined the longstanding Democratic policy of free trade, low tariffs, with the Whig Party policy of internal improvements—infrastructure designed to hasten the advance of Americans to the Pacific coast. The Young Americans attempted to settle the slavery controversy that threatened the Union by valorizing popular sovereignty in a way the American Founders had not done. The Founders' regime located sovereignty in the people, but the people must adhere to the greater sovereignty of the laws of Nature and of

Nature's God; by proposing that newly-acquired territories west of the Mississippi River vote slavery up or down, then be admitted as new states of the Union on the basis of that majority decision, and by professing not to care which way they chose, Senator Douglas and New America generally were "blowing out the moral lights around us," as Abraham Lincoln would charge in 1858. They were arguing that majority rule, a form of might and not moral law, made right. But the boundless sea, where might makes rights, can be ruled only by Leviathan, the mightiest of the mighty. This would bring America to Hobbes and absolute monarchy in principle, if not immediately in practice.

Melville initially supported Young America, publishing in its main literary journal, the *Democratic Review*.[3] But by the time he wrote *Moby-Dick* he had become increasingly disenchanted; in his subsequent novel, a parody of the life of Jesus entitled *Pierre; or, The Ambiguities*, he would deride *literary* Young America as too genteel, too 'idealistic' about 'the democracy,' the people of America. His Ishmael, in but no longer of American society because he had experienced the searing events of shipwreck, functions as a prophetic witness to Americans, 'young' or not. The great nation he would found will understand God and nature much differently than any Americans had hitherto done. This new nation would reject both Christianity and then-fashionable Transcendentalism as 'idealizing' veils over the chaotic waters that surround and, in the fiery form of molten rock undergird the seemingly stable land. At the same time, Americans would also reject the insane quest to rule chaos, a quest that causes the would-be conqueror to imitate his intended prey in his self-destructive, and regime-destructive, malice disguised as moral outrage. And although it would not reject commerce as a way of life, it would know that peaceful commerce isn't all there is to human life and nature, human or otherwise.

Given his intellectual and moral distance from much of existing American doctrine, Ishmael adopts the irony if not necessarily the dialectic of Socrates. He offers his readers a lighthearted account of going to sea to counteract 'the blues' or, as he calls it, "the hypoes." "With a philosophical

---

3  For an account of Melville and the Young America movement, see Andrew Delbanco: *Melville: His World and His Work* (New York: Vintage Books, 2005), 95–96.

flourish Cato throws himself upon his sword; I quietly take to the ship."
Moreover, "all men"—the democracy itself—"cherish nearly the same feelings from time to time," longing to get away from civil society to think, to
dream, to be "wild." In New York City, people interrupt their commercial
busy-ness to stare at the sea "with ocean reveries," congregating along the
shore as "crowds of water-gazers" (795). In the countryside they gravitate
to lakes and streams, for the same reason. "Meditation and water are wed-
ded forever" in the minds of artists, poets, and boys (796). Religious men,
too, from the Persians to the Greeks, seek the water (although as readers
will see, Persians also seek the fire). Ishmael doesn't mention the waters of
Christian baptism, but they cannot be far from his mind. But in these med-
itations the seekers find not God but themselves. Water reflects; "[W]e see
ourselves in all rivers and oceans." Narcissus drowns, seeking "the image of
the ungraspable phantom of life," "the key to it all" (797). The breath of
life, the "H" in the whale, does not lend itself to human control. Proverbially the individual in love with himself, Narcissus illustrates the perils of
self-love as it gazes at life and sees only itself. Ishmael will almost drown at
sea, but not quite; water or life absorbs the self-absorbed, but Ishmael isn't
entirely self-absorbed and so he survives.

Continuing his *apologia* for his conduct, Ishmael remarks that he goes
to sea not as a passenger (he has no money), nor as an officer (for as a *former*
schoolmaster, "I abominate all honorable respectable toils, trials and tribu-
lations whatsoever"). "It is quite as much as I can do to take care of myself"
(797). He does take care of himself but doesn't mind being ruled by others
on ship. As a sailor, he must follow orders. But the New Testament tells us
to accept our station in life, however menial, and for that matter, "Who
ain't a slave?" Every human being gets thumped "either in a physical or
metaphysical" way (798). Metaphysical democracy or egalitarian thumping
prevails over all; Being itself pushes all of us around. Having thus vindicated
his honor as one who is ruled and not the ruler, Ishmael addresses the needs
of the body. Unlike passengers, sailors get paid. The "urbane activity with
which a man receives money" shows up either the self-contradiction or the
hypocrisy of Christians, who believe the love of money to be the root of all
evil. "Ah! How cheerfully we consign ourselves to perdition!" (798–799)
The common sailor's body benefits not only from the human artifact of
money but from "the wholesome exercise and pure air of the forecastle

deck," from nature and benefits he gains to a greater degree than his ruler, the Commodore on the quarter-deck, standing as he is behind the forecastle deck. Does the putative ruler really rule at all? Just as the Commodore only thinks he breathes fresh air, but really breathes air already breathed by the sailors, "in much the same way do the commonalty lead their leaders in many other things, at the same time that the leaders little suspect it." And finally, what rules them all, if not "the invisible police officer of the Fates"? They are the ones who "cajol[ed] me into the delusion that [going to sea] was a choice resulting from my own unbiased freewill and discriminating judgment." In calling the Fates "stage managers," Ishmael invokes neither the Bible nor human conquest, but the ancient pagan Greek claim that even the gods are the ruled and not the rulers (799). The Fates weave the destinies of gods and human beings alike. They are the ultimate 'loomers.'

Having so determined, or having been so determined, playful and ironic Ishmael immediately lists his principal motive for going to sea on a whaling ship: "the overwhelming idea of the great whale himself." "Such a portentous"—looming—"and mysterious monster aroused all my curiosity" (799–800). Ishmael's motto might be, "I wander because I wonder.'" If for the Bible's prophets fear of God is the beginning of wisdom, for philosophers wonder is. But to wonder is to wonder at things beyond the land, beyond civil society; it is to become a "wild man" of sorts, an Ishmael in the modern world, in America. Wonderers and wanderers push beyond civil boundaries or conventions. "I am tormented with an everlasting itch for things remote. I love to sail forbidden seas, and land on barbarous coasts. Not ignoring what is good"—in this he differs from his ruler aboard ship, Captain Ahab—"I am quick to perceive a horror, and could still be social with it—would they let me—since it is but well to be on friendly terms with all the inmates of the place one lodges in" (800).

And so it is with the water, with the surface of chaos; "the great flood-gates of the wonder-world swung wide open" to a voyage in which two "wild conceits" "swayed me to my purpose," floating "in my inmost soul": They are the "endless processions of the whale," that king of the boundless sea, "and, midmost of them all, one grand hooded phantom, like a snow hill in the air" (800). Moby-Dick, the snow-white king of all kings of the boundless sea, appears for the first time in this yarn not in the mind of Ahab, whom the Whale obsesses, but in the mind of Ishmael. Ishmael knows about the white whale before he meets Ahab, before embarking on the voyage of the *Pequod*. This is the invisible mind-link between captain and sailor, ruler and ruled, the one who wants to close in on the white whale to destroy it, the other who wants to close in on the white whale to understand and in some sense to befriend it. The mother of the Biblical Ishmael addresses God as *El Roy*—"God of seeing" or "Thou God seest me," understand me. The modern Ishmael wants to see, not to kill, perhaps to be seen, and surely not to be killed. Americans too need to come to terms with the white whale if they are to perceive reality as it is without bringing destruction upon themselves.

## Chapter Two
# THE ADVENTURE BEFORE
# THE ADVENTURE

Ishmael intends to sail from Nantucket, the "great original" of American whaling, where local Amerindians first ventured on to the water to hunt Leviathan (801). In returning to the point of whaling's genesis in what would become the United States of his lifetime, Ishmael reminds himself and his readers that the hunt predates the arrival of Europeans here. The hunt began before the 'age of exploration,' modernity and capitalism. The hunt is human, not time-bound or 'culture'-bound.

It is December and it is cold. He stops in New Bedford, another whaling town, to spend the night before proceeding to Nantucket. His search for cheap lodging on the freezing night takes on a boundaries-pushing, slightly phantasmagorical character as he wanders from hotel to hotel, even stumbling into the local black church, where pilgrim and parishioners behold one another with mutual surprise and incomprehension. Arriving finally at the Spouter Inn, he remarks the irony of the proprietor's name, Peter Coffin; the rock of this establishment hardly invokes eternal life. (As events come to pass at the end of the yarn, a coffin will nonetheless save him, as this Coffin saves him from frostbite.) Ishmael reminds himself of Lazarus, the beggar at the doorstep of the rich man in Luke 16, self-pityingly imagining that even Lazarus did not need to suffer through a freezing New England winter. But he immediately recalls himself to his mission and enters the inn.

There he sees an oil painting done in dark, Turneresque shades, seemingly an attempt by the artist "to delineate chaos bewitched," to control chaos rather in the way of the witches on the blasted heat in *Macbeth*. Sublime if not beautiful, the painting "froze you to it"—doing to the mind what a Massachusetts winter does to the body—"till you involuntarily took an oath with yourself to find out what [it] meant" (805). Ishmael cannot be sure, but he comes to "a final theory of my own," that the picture represents a ship sailing around Cape Horn in a hurricane, with "an exasperated whale, purposing to spring clean over the craft [...] in the enormous act of impaling itself upon the three mastheads" (806). Destruction of both ship and whale, hunter and hunted; chaos come again, as a Shakespearean character might say. Having reached one of those boundary lines he had determined to test, "I resolved to spend the rest of the evening as a looker-on," a man who wants to see (808).

A crew newly arrived from a whaling expedition is the first thing to see. As the men drink and caper at the bar, Ishmael notices a man named Bulkington, a Southerner. He too has separated himself from the company, looking on. Soon he discreetly separates himself from the scene altogether; when his mates notice his absence they go in search of him. They respect him, perhaps as a natural ruler or aristocrat. He will sign on with the *Pequod* expedition, but will attract little notice on that ship, which will remain firmly in the hands of a tyrant. In socially egalitarian or democratic America, aristocrats natural and artificial do not rule. Jefferson and Adams had hoped that natural *aristoi*, such as themselves, would continue to rule America, esteemed by their fellow citizens. Subsequent generations would need to rule on their own and the quasi-aristocrat South would soon attempt to separate itself from the Union. As for natural aristocrats, there is a place for them, sometimes, in small portions of American society, but they will not rule the New America. Both aristocrats who no longer rule and inquirers who will never rule but simply want to see must separate themselves to some degree from the people.

Landlord Coffin offers to rent Ishmael a room and a bed, both to be shared with a harpooneer who, Coffin cheerfully reports, is at the moment out trying to sell the last shrunken head he'd acquired on a voyage to New Zealand—New Bedford being a commercial town, after all, and America a commercial republic. (It should not go unnoticed that commercial transactions require not only a willing seller but a willing buyer, and Queequeg has been selling shrunken heads to the local Christians.) Coffin assures Ishmael that the bed was his marital bed, big enough for two. Unassured by the arrangement, Ishmael retires, awakened by the sight of Queequeg, tattooed from head to foot, surely "some abominable savage or other shipped aboard of a whaleman in the south Seas, and so landed in this Christian country." Foreshadowing his encounters with several Quakers in the months to come, Ishmael shudders: "I quaked to think of it." He calms himself somewhat by thinking, "It's only his outside. A man can be honest in any sort of skin." He tells himself this homily doesn't quite work, as fear returns; yet, as he insists, "the parent of fear" is ignorance (816). If the Bible teaches that fear of God is the beginning of wisdom, Ishmael counters that ignorance of men is the parent of fear; hence his boundary-pushing, his quest for knowledge. Indeed, these chapters of the novel show Ishmael succeeding in overcoming fear and getting "on friendly terms" with the tattooed, idolatrous, shrunken-head-selling cannibal with whom he will spend this night.

After some mutual alarm and a timely intervention by Mr. Coffin, Queequeg takes the measure of his new roommate and commands him to get into the bed. "He really did this in not only a civil but a really kind and charitable way"; accordingly, Ishmael tells himself, "the man's a human being just as I am: he has just as much reason to fear me, as I have to be afraid of him. Better sleep with a sober cannibal than a drunken Christian" (818–819). Having "never slept better in his life," in this new bed in New Bedford, Ishmael awakens the next morning to find himself in "the comical predicament" of having sleeping Queequeg's massive arms around him—a bit more of a marital bed than either had planned (820). This recalls Ishmael to a childhood incident when he was sent to bed by his stepmother as punishment and dreamed that "a supernatural hand was placed in mine." Real or imagined, the sensation, puzzles him "to this day" (821). But the current dilemma is natural enough, and after finally awakening his bedmate he resumes his role as looker-on, for Queequeg "and his ways were well worth unusual regarding" (822). He concludes that Queequeg is no savage but rather "just civilized enough to show off his outlandishness in the strangest possible manner," dressing himself from the head down, for example, and shaving himself with the edge of his harpoon's steel head (823). They go down to breakfast, where the landlord regards Ishmael with the amusement of a congenial prankster, a comic matchmaker. Ishmael doesn't mind: "A good laugh is a mighty good thing, and rather too scarce a good thing." No need for wounded pride at being laughed at. "The man that has anything bountifully laughable about him, be sure there is more in that man than you perhaps think for"—an aphorism equally applicable to Quee-queg and Ishmael himself (825). His future tyrant-captain, Ahab, will sometimes laugh, but never at himself. The whalemen eat their breakfast in silence, punctuated by Queequeg's spearing of lightly-cooked steaks with his harpoon.

Thus cheered, Ishmael finds more comedy in the streets of New Bed-ford, where he strolls later that morning. It turns out that Queequeg isn't so unusual here, as "in New Bedford, actual cannibals stand chatting at street corners; savages outright; many of whom yet carry on their bones unholy flesh." "Still more curious, certainly more comical," are the young New Englanders in town to sign on for a whaling voyage, "all athirst for gain and glory in the fishery" (827). In New Bedford, the Americans are in some ways as outlandish as the savages—in a way, even more so, as they have yet to go to sea. Americans and foreigners alike contrast with the men who invest in the ships, men as wealthy as any in America, whose wealth enables them to "superinduce bright terraces of flowers upon the barren re-fuse rocks thrown aside at creation's final day" (829). Ishmael had arrived on Saturday night, just before the Sabbath commemorating God's day of rest after creation, and now sees the seeming omnipotence of human art to transform that creation. Foreign savages, green boys from the Green Moun-tains, and prosperous merchants all seek the conquest of the nature that gives them little to work with. Ishmael will watch them try; Ahab will chan-nel their energies into another, wilder quest. And so to church.

Ishmael enters the Whaleman's Chapel. The Chapel is for whalemen, their wives, and their widows, who sit apart from one another, "as if each silent grief were insular and incommunicable" (830). This is the second ap-pearance in the novel of human beings closed off from one another—"isola-toes," as Ishmael will later call them—the silent sailors at breakfast being the first. Awaiting the preacher, the parishioners solemnly read plaques on the wall memorializing dead sailors, each reader recalling her own dead, or con-sidering his own possible death at sea. They find no consolation in what they read, only more intense isolation in suffering or in fear. Tocqueville, too, had seen what he called the "individualism" brought on by democracy, the con-dition of social equality; he had observed that Americans combatted its melancholy by forming civil associations, strengthening citizenship. Melville sees the condition without seeing any evidence of countervailing fellowship.

Aside from Ishmael, the only one present who pays attention to the others is Queequeg, who sits with "a wondering gaze of incredulous curiosity in his countenance"; Queequeg is a 'wonderer' as well as a 'wanderer' and in this resembles Ishmael (831). In his case, however, wondering without believing comes from an inability to read; reading physically isolates the reader from his surroundings, including other people, and it will transpire that reading pious inscriptions and even the Bible can prove isolating, too. "What deadly voids and unbidden infidelities in the lines that seem to gnaw upon all Faith, and refuse resurrections to the beings who have placeless perished without a grave," in unconsecrated groundlessness (832).

In all this Ishmael detects contradiction in Christian souls. If we really believe that the dead now dwell "in unspeakable bliss," why do we mourn them? Either our faith is weak, or the Biblical promise of immortality is an illusion. "But Faith, like a jackal, feeds among the tombs, and even from these dead doubts she gathers her most vital hope"—perhaps the hope of seeing the departed loved one, again (832). Does Faith bring eternal life, through God's grace? The biblical Ishmael is the one *not* among those chosen by God, and Melville's Ishmael will fare no better, spiritually, even if he does find physical salvation and uses it to serve as a witness.

Ishmael thinks, "the same fate may be thine." Despite this prospect of death at sea, "somehow I grew merry again," not through faith in salvation by God but through nature conceived Socratically. "Methinks we have hugely mistaken this matter of Life and Death." If "what they call my shadow here on earth is my true substance," and if our bodies prevent us from clearly seeing "things spiritual," then "my body is but the lees of my better being"; when death takes my body, it won't take me. Death is like a wound that punctures a barrel, releasing the wine. Death will "stave" my soul; the pun on "save" also includes a double thought on the barrel, inasmuch as staving refers not only to barrels but to ships, which sink when staved, bringing soul-liberating death to those on board (833).

The whalemen call the preacher "Father" Mapple, respecting him as Catholics respect a priest, although he is a Protestant. The Whaleman's Chapel refers not only to the congregation but also to him, as he too has hunted whales. Neither Ishmael nor Melville himself could dismiss him as a landlubber, a man clueless concerning the harsh and chaotic sea and its denizens. On land, he still retains the habits of a sailor, arriving after walking to his church in the freezing rain, little concerned with his own comfort. 'I am your captain, the Bible our orders, God our admiral,' his demeanor seems to say.

Before recalling the sermon, Ishmael describes two more features of the church. One is a painting. In contrast to the entirely dark painting at the Spouter-Inn, this picture shows an angel with a radiant, sun-like face, over-looking a ship. The guardian angel replaces the destroying angel, the whale hovering over the masts of the ship. The other feature is the pulpit, modeled on a mainmast, complete with a rope-ladder. Ishmael understands this sym-bolically: "[T]he world's a ship on its passage out, and not a voyage com-plete: and the pulpit is its prow." Thus, the pulpit "leads the world" (836). Father Mapple offers Ishmael an alternative captaincy to that of Ahab.

The service begins with a hymn. American literature scholar David H. Battenfield identifies this as an adaptation of a hymn sung in the Reformed Protestant Dutch Church, the church Melville had attended with his mother.[4] But the hymn sung in the Whaleman's Chapel has all references to Jesus removed. Father Mapple does indeed speak for God the Father, not the Son, offering an interpretation of the Old Testament story of Jonah and the whale. There, Jonah (whose name means "dove," carrier of mes-sages) disobeys God who commands him to go to Nineveh and prophesy against "their wickedness" (Jonah 1:1). Fearing for his life if he were to go among such men, contradicting the meaning of his name, Jonah disobeys, paying ship passage to Tarshish instead. God sends a storm; the sailors in-terrogate Jonah and learn that he is fleeing God. They call out to God to spare them, as they are innocents. To appease God, they throw Jonah into the sea, where he's swallowed by "a great fish" (1:16). From the belly of the beast Jonah prays for deliverance; God does deliver him, and he proceeds obediently to Nineveh. Far from being killed, Jonah succeeds; the Ninevites repent, and God repents of His intention to destroy them. Angry with God for sparing the evil Ninevites, Jonah relents when God teaches him to dis-criminate between the good and the evil, the innocent and the guilty. Not all of the Ninevites are guilty, and the many who were have now repented of their evil ways.

4    David H. Battenfield, "The Source of the Hymn in *Moby-Dick*," in *America Literature*, XXVII (November 1955) 393–396.

Father Mapple interprets the yarn. "If we obey God, we must disobey ourselves; and it is in this disobeying ourselves, wherein the harness of obeying God consists" (838). Like the Ninevites, Jonah much prefers to disobey God and follow his own lead. "Jonah sought to flee world-wide from God" (839); he might resemble some of the sailors, indeed Ishmael, although unlike Jonah Ishmael does not pay his own way. Mapple says that the fugitive Jonah's conscience provides his first punishment, torturing him spiritually while aboard the ship. But he confesses to the sailors. They initially show him mercy, turning first to prayer and only then to action when God chooses not to answer their prayer. Mapple adds to the Biblical account with a vivid description of Jonah sinking into the sea and the jaws of the whale, then describes Jonah's prayer from the whale's belly as repentant, not self-justifying. "And here, shipmates, is true and faithful repentance; not clamorous for pardon, but grateful for punishment." In retelling and embellishing the Biblical yarn, Mapple exhibits "an aspect of the deepest yet manliest humility" (844). He could never be considered a poor-spirited or 'effeminate' Christian of the sort Machiavelli derided.

Mapple then draws his final lessons from the yarn: "[P]reach the Truth in the face of Falsehood"; and, turning now to himself especially, "woe to the pilot of the living God who slights it" by succumbing to the "charms" of the world instead of adhering to "Gospel duty." "Woe to him who seeks to please rather than to appall! Woe to him whose name is more to him than goodness! Woe to him who, in this world, courts not dishonor! Woe to him who would not be true, even though to be false were salvation!" Such a pilot, such a seeker of popularity and honor, a man who would lie to save his life, fails to follow the example of "the great Pilot Paul," eventually a martyr for God. Such a false pilot, "while preaching to others is himself a castaway!" (845) Father Mapple is preaching to himself, examining his own soul and finding it sinful. He is, after all, a man who ascends to a mast-like pulpit, and evidently makes no objection to being called "Father" by his listeners. He attempts to rally his spirits, saying that not misery but "Delight—top-gallant delight is to him, who acknowledges no law or lord, but the Lord his God, and is only patriot to heaven" (845). He tells his congregation and perhaps most of all himself that the patriot of the Kingdom of God will find joy, unlike the patriot of any kingdom of man. He blesses the congregation; they depart, "and he was left alone in the place"

(845). However impressive and moving, the Bible message has united neither the congregants with one another nor the messenger with his congregants. Is this dilemma following from the absence of Christ from the sermon, or does it follow, in Ishmael's and perhaps Melville's judgment, from the radically unnatural teaching of the Bible itself? Does it follow from the fact that an Israelite could unite his patriotism on this earth with his patriotism as a citizen of God's Kingdom (since Israel was God's Kingdom), whereas a Christian can do no such thing—that is, not with God's sanction? However it may be, the sermon's message prefigures Ishmael's own testimony, which appalls instead of pleases, aiming not at popularity but at truth as he sees it.

Ishmael returns to the Spouter-Inn to find Queequeg, like Father Mapple, "quite alone," having left the Whaleman's Chapel before the benediction (846). Like the preacher, he attends to religious obsequies, busying himself with his idol. Although Ishmael finds Queequeg's face hideous, "his countenance yet had a something in it which was by no means disagreeable. You cannot hide the soul." Honesty, courage, nobility, and liberty: His head "reminded me of George Washington's head." "Queequeg was George Washington cannibalistically developed" (846–847). The underlying nature of human types shines out from the tattoos of convention, custom. Initially "overawing" (the 'H', again), "savages" or men close to nature exhibit "calm self-collectedness or simplicity" evincing "a Socratic wisdom." Queequeg is a man of nature, a sort of philosopher, in contrast with Father Mapple, whose God commands us to resist our (fallen) nature. Thousands of miles from his home, "thrown among people as strange to him as though he were on the planet Jupiter," Queequeg nonetheless "seemed entirely at his ease; preserving the utmost serenity; content with his own companionship; always equal to himself. Surely this was a touch of fine philosophy [...]" (847). Has Father Mapple achieved the delight he hopes for? Or the serenity? He might answer, 'No, nor shall I, this side of the coffin's lid.'

On this cold December night, Ishmael felt "a melting in me." "No more my splintered heart and maddened hand were turned against the wolfish world. This soothing savage had redeemed it." Ishmael finds himself redeemed not by Mapple's religion but by Queequeg's philosophic character, "speaking a nature in which there lurked no civilized hypocrisies and bland deceits." He decides, "I'll try a pagan friend [...] since Christian kindness has proved but hollow courtesy." They "left as cronies," "naturally and unbiddenly"—that is, with no need for commands divine or human. Queequeg announced that "henceforth we were married," meaning "we were bosom friends" (848). He presents Ishmael with the shrunken head and half his money as gifts—charitable by nature, Christian without Christianity. Ishmael syllogizes theologically: surely the "magnanimous God of heaven and earth" could not possibly "be jealous of an insignificant bit of black wood," Queequeg's idol. Given that worship is to do the will of God, and that "God wills to do to my fellow man what I would have my fellow man to do to me," since Queequeg is "my fellow man," why would Ishmael not want to reciprocate his attendance at a Christian religious service with my assistance in kindling the shavings he burns in homage to his "innocent little idol"? He even lets Queequeg smoke in bed: "How elastic our stiff prejudices become when love comes to bend them."[5] Such elasticity likely increases when the reasoner adroitly selects which of God's commands he disobeys (the prohibition against idolatry) and which he obeys (the Golden Rule); there may be more sophistry than Socrateity in Ishmael's syllogism, but there is no lack of Socratic playfulness.

In a further Socratic/Platonic touch, the natural philosopher turns out also to be a potential king, the son of a Pacific island chief and nephew of a high priest. He left the island to "learn among the Christians"—to learn both their arts and their religion. "But alas! The practices of whalemen soon convinced him that even Christians could be both miserable and wicked; infinitely more so, than all his father's heathens" (857). Going against nature can produce prodigies of both good and evil: Scripture stokes the grandest ambitions, whether it is the Apostle Paul's mission to bring the Gospel to the nations or Milton's Satan's defiant preference for ruling in Hell instead of serving in Heaven. Ishmael (and Melville) make it plain,

---

5    Given the imagery of marriage Melville deploys to describe the friendship of Ishmael and Queequeg, several commentators have alleged that their relationship is sexual. The method deployed to consider the evidence for this is dubious, consisting of taking several passages in ways that confuse intimacy with sex. What Melville actually does, very characteristically, is to leave matters in a state of ambiguity, suggesting a sense of testing if not crossing the boundaries, very much in the manner that Ishmael valorized at the beginning of his yarn.

through Queequeg's testimony, that religious customs are indeed customary, conventional—a characteristic teaching of the philosophers. Ishmael sets himself against convention, against the ways of landsmen: "How I spurned the turnpike earth!—that common highway all over dented with the marks of slavish heels and hoofs; and turned me to admire the magnanimity of the sea [...]" (857). Philosophy and (aristocratic) morality—the magnanimity that serves as the crown of the classical virtues—both beckon him, as he chooses the natural friendship offered by Queequeg against the unnatural, isolating revealed religion of Father Mapple; fraternity wins his soul, not fatherly authority. As they are ferried from New Bedford to Nantucket, their fellow passengers "marveled that two fellow beings should be so companionable, as though a white man were anything more dignified than a whitewashed negro" (857); natural equality undergirds natural friendship. It is now no wonder that Jesus had been excluded from the hymn and the sermon at the Whaleman's Inn: The brotherly, down-to-earth Person of God who obeys the Father's Command to die on the Cross combines fraternity and the authority of fatherhood, calling into question the dichotomy Melville wants to establish.

*Chapter Three*

# THE SHIP AND ITS RULERS

Queequeg's idol 'tells' him that Ishmael should select the ship they will sail on. The idol will prove a poor adviser, but off Ishmael goes. He settles on the *Pequod*—named, somewhat ominously, after a Massachusetts Indian tribe now extinct. It's "a ship of the old school," well-weathered, "a cannibal of a craft"—in that way resembling his new friend—"tricking herself forth in the chased bones of her enemies." Also like Queequeg, it is "a noble craft," but unlike him "a most melancholy one" (867–868). "All noble things touched in that" (868)—a sentiment recalling Napoleon's remark, "Yes, it is sad, like greatness."[6] Greatness is sad because it is solitary; the great, by definition, must have few peers. The noble melancholy of the *Pequod* anticipates the character of Ahab, not Queequeg. Such a solid old craft, decorated with souvenirs of past triumphs over its prey, may attract Ishmael, giving him what will turn out to be a false sense of security. But he gives his readers no explicit reason for his decision, which may relate to his interest in seeking the origins of things.

He discovers one of the ship's two principal owners, Captain Peleg, in his office—a wigwam on the deck, recalling the tribal name of the ship and,

---

6    Trained as a lawyer, Pierre-Louis Roederer read and admired Adam Smith's *The Wealth of Nations*. He specialized in commercial and tax law, serving as a Council of State and Senator under Napoleon. Walking with the Emperor at the gloomy Tuileries Palace, Roederer ventured to say that the place was sad. "Yes, it is sad, like greatness," Napoleon replied. Charles de Gaulle interpreted this to mean that the great man, in taking supreme responsibility for a battle, or for the ship of state, necessarily isolates himself from those who do not take such responsibility. If that is what Napoleon meant, in associating greatness with noble melancholy he separated himself from, and elevated himself above, the disciples of Smith, for whom commerce betokened the natural sociality of human nature. Ahab will soon separate himself from the cheerful, businesslike Quakerism of his second mate, Mr. Stubb.

in the minds of some commentators, the symbol of the Democratic Party's Tammany Hall organization (and if so intended, a reminder of Young America). The owners and officers of the *Pequod* are Quakers, although each has gone his separate way from the original doctrines of the sect. Peleg tests the young volunteer. He disdains Ishmael's merchant-marine background—no preparation for whaling—and asks him why he wants to go on the hunt. To learn about whaling and to see the world, Ishmael replies, to which Peleg counters, if you want to "know what whaling is," look at the ship captain, Ahab, who lost his leg to a whale, and if you want to see the world the way a whaler sees it, just look out at the ocean from right here because that is what you'll be seeing from aboard ship (869). Ishmael persists, which is all Peleg really cares about: his resolve.

The other principal owner, Captain Bildad, himself has captained a whale ship. He presents a paradox: He is a pacifist engaged in a highly sanguinary occupation. Such men "are fighting Quakers, they are Quakers with a vengeance," named "with Scripture names," speaking with the 'thees' and 'thous' of Quaker households, but "strangely blend[ing] with these unoutgrown peculiarities, a thousand bold dashes of character, not unworthy a Scandinavian sea-king, or a poetical Pagan Roman" (872). Now looking back at his then-future captain, Ishmael remarks that "when these things unite in a man of greatly superior natural force, with a globular brain and a ponderous heart," long at sea and thus far from the conventions of shore, that man comes "to think untraditionally and independently; receiving all nature's sweet or savage impressions fresh from their own virgin, voluntary, and confiding breast." Such a man may "learn a bold and nervous lofty language"—like Ahab, and indeed like Melville. Combined, these attributes make him "one in a whole nation's census—a mighty pageant creature, formed for noble tragedies." "If either by birth or by circumstances, he have what seems a half willful over-ruling morbidness at the bottom of his nature"—intensifying the sadness of greatness—he will indeed be "another phase of the Quaker" (872). The unresolvable tension between Christianity, especially in its Quaker form, and the warrior spirit, combined with intellectual brilliance, great-heartedness, experience of many civilizations that are far from Christian, exposure to the violent self-contradictions of the natural world; a gift of eloquence and therefore persuasiveness; and an obsession with death, the unbreachable limit of all these qualities: this man may turn tyrant, but he will be no ordinary tyrant. He will become, as it were, a metaphysical tyrant, a tyrant who takes his subjects on voyages of carnage. Stalin once said to de Gaulle: "In the end, death is the only winner." If so, will not such a man not want to situate himself on the side of death?

In the meantime, more mundane considerations prevail. Peleg and Bildad negotiate over how little they will pay Ishmael. Bildad's Quakerism has given itself over not to tyranny but to business. "Very probably he had long since come to the sage and sensible conclusion that a man's religion is one thing, and this practical world quite another. This world pays dividends" (873). Indeed, "For a pious man, especially for a Quaker, he was certainly rather hard-hearted, to say the least"—never swearing except when he was aboard ship commanding his men, from whom he "got an inordinate quantity of cruel, unmitigated hard work" (873). This is the Quakerism of Benjamin Franklin's Philadelphia, grown up in what had been Puritan Massachusetts, a Quakerism that has generated in Bildad a "utilitarian character" (873). The sea takes men away from the metes and bounds of land, but the way one acts when at sea, when liberated from the conventions of landedness, testifies to the nature of one's soul. And souls will be seen to differ from the conventions they adopt when souls' natures are made manifest.

Peleg's Quakerism, somewhat less hard, has turned toward the valetudinarian. Captain Ahab, he explains, is "a grand, ungodly, god-like man," but a young sailor shouldn't worry. True, he's named for the tyrant of 1 Kings 16–27, a man "evil in the sight of the LORD," a Baal-worshipper who "did more to provoke the LORD of Israel than all the kings of Israel that were before him" (16:33), a man who fights three battles against the Syrians and dies during the last one, and to the end the enemy of the prophet Elijah. But really, Peleg insists, Ahab's "a good man," "something like me—only there's a good deal more of him." Admittedly, "he was out of his mind for a spell," but only because his wound caused him such pain. "Ever since he lost his leg last voyage by that accursed whale, he's been kind of moody—desperate moody, and savage sometimes; but that will all pass off." Peleg concludes, sententiously, that "it's better to sail with a moody good captain than a laughing bad one," and besides, Ahab has a "sweet, resigned" young wife and a child. (Does she attend Father Mapple's church?

Did Ishmael see her, without knowing who she was?) "Ahab has his humanities!" (879) Peleg will prove no better a prophet than Queequeg's idol, although he is more loquacious. Ishmael goes away feeling "a sympathy and a sorrow" and also "a sort of awe"—the 'H' again (879). His good experience with the noble savage Queequeg (better to sleep with a sober cannibal than a drunken Christian) and his turning away from Biblical restraints inclines him to underestimate the danger of the civilized, if sometime-savage captain, one might think, although it is not clear that Melville so thinks.

Ishmael returns to the inn, finding Queequeg in the midst of a fast, perhaps as a precautionary act of devotion before the voyage to come. Ishmael delivers himself of a characteristically American rumination on religious tolerance. "We good Presbyterian Christians should be charitable in these things, and not fan cy ourselves so vastly superior to other mortals, pagans and what not, because of their half-crazy conceits on these subjects." Queequeg is content to worship his idol and fast; "[T]here let him rest." No one will argue him out of his beliefs, and truth be told "we are all somehow dreadfully cracked about the head, and sadly need mending." The limits Ishmael puts on toleration are killing or insulting others and injury to oneself (880). Wondering if the fast has weakened Queequeg, he finds himself assured that his friend suffers from no dyspepsia on account of it; indeed, his only experience of stomach upset occurred back on the island, when he over-ate at a barbecue of slain enemy corpses—protein passed around "just as though these presents were so many Christmas turkeys," which one supposes also may cause similar discomfort (885). Ishmael doubts that "my remarks about religion made much impression upon Queequeg," who "seem[ed] dull of hearing on that important subject, unless considered from his own point of view," a not uncommon trait among the pious. Also, he "did not more than one third understand me," perhaps because of the language barrier. He finally "looked at me with a sort of condescending concern and compassion, as though he thought it a great pity that such a sensible young man should be so hopelessly lost to evangelical pagan piety" (885).

As for Quakers Peleg and Bildad, their theological concerns prove simpler than Ishmael's; they overcome any religious scruples about signing Queequeg as a harpooneer when they see how well he can throw his weapon. Indeed, when Bildad offers him a Bible tract, Peleg admonishes him: "Pious harpooneers never make good voyages—it takes the shark out of 'em" (888–891). Heaven forfend. For his part, Bildad corrects Peleg's suggestion that he and Ahab must have thought of death and God's judgment when in storms at sea; they thought of what actions would save their lives and the lives of their crew. For these Quakers, physical concerns readily supersede spiritual ones, self-help prayer.

Ishmael remains in the grip of a feebler form of self-help—namely, wishful thinking, or more accurately, wishful thoughtlessness. Back in Nantucket, before the final boarding, he is approached by a man calling himself Elijah—the name of the Biblical prophet who opposes Ahab and Jezebel—who issues vague warnings about Captain Ahab. "I pronounced him in my heart, a humbug," a false prophet, Ishmael recalls. Still, Ishmael had his doubts about "commit[ting] myself this way to so long a voyage without once laying my eyes on the man who was to be the absolute dictator of it," but "when a man suspects any wrong, it sometimes happens that if he be already involved in the matter, he insensibly strives to cover up his suspicions even from himself." And so he "said nothing, and tried to think nothing" (896). When in doubt, he denies.

Upon returning to the ship, he and Queequeg learn that Ahab has boarded it. They set sail on Christmas day, listening to Bildad sing a hymn "full of hope and fruition" (903). Bulkington is on board, too, and Ishmael pays retrospective tribute to his now-dead shipmate, a natural aristocrat who preferred "the open independence of the sea" to "the treacherous, slavish shore." "As in landlessness alone resides the highest truth, shoreless, indefinite as God—so, better is it to perish in that howling infinite, than be ingloriously dashed upon the lee, even if that were safety!" (906) In a chapter titled "The Advocate" Ishmael expands this thought by making a sort of lawyer's case in defense of whaling. Yes, it is a butchering business, but so is war, and we honor the warrior spirit of "Martial Commanders"; aristocrats in their own way, whalers show the greatest courage, for "What are the comprehensible terrors of men compared to the interlinked terrors of God!" (909) Commerce, discovery, the political liberation of Latin America, the light that glows in religious shrines, the Kantian-philosophic prospect of world peace by dint of mutual understanding of civilized and savage peoples—all these great goods, real and prospective, owe a debt to whaling, a vocation praised by great authors from Job to Edmund Burke. The whale has even been written in the stars, as seen in the constellation Cetus. Don't take your hat off in the presence of the Czar, but rather to Queequeg. And as for the life of the mind, "A whale-ship was my Yale College and my Harvard." (912)

The thought of Bulkington has put Ishmael in an aristocratic frame of mind, and the loquacity which has followed overwhelms his reservations about subjecting himself to the regime of a tyrant. Unlike Father Mapple's sermon, his rhetoric has persuaded its principal audience, the orator himself. As for Bulkington, commentators have wondered why he never opposes the rule of Ahab, as aristocrats have opposed tyrants. Neither Ishmael nor Melville explains this, but there may have been a hint in the earlier chapter in which Bulkington was introduced. At the inn, he does not attempt to rule his unruly and vulgar comrades; he could, because when he leaves, they follow him. But he does leave, likely tired of their carousing. Bulkington's aristocratic distaste for the *vulgus*, 'the people,' may hold him back from acting to protect them, from moving decisively against tyranny that issues from the American regime, which valorizes the people. This suggests that Melville might view with skepticism Tocqueville's noble appeal to European nobles to guide the people as societies democratize.

No tyrant can rule alone. He needs not a real aristocracy but a pseudo-aristocracy that will enforce his commands and require of him no Magna Carta. Ishmael sketches portraits of Ahab's three officers: the first mate, Starbuck; the second mate, Stubb; the third mate, Flask. While Ahab captains the ship, each of them captains one of the three boats lowered at the sighting of a whale. A Quaker from Nantucket, "a long, earnest man," "a staid, steadfast man," Starbuck proves "uncommonly conscientious for a seaman," "endued with deep natural reverence"—perhaps the Quaker "inner light" (914). And a prudent one, saying, "I will have no man in my boat who is not afraid of a whale," apparently meaning "not only that the most reliable and useful courage is that which arises from the fair estimation of the encountered peril, but that an utterly fearless man is a far more dangerous comrade than a coward" (915). If fear of God is the beginning of wisdom for Starbuck as a Christian, fear of the whale is its beginning for Starbuck as a whaler. His nature inclines him not only to the reverence befitting a Quaker but to what might be described as an Aristotelian esteem for the *metrion*, the moral center between impassioned extremes. Having lost his father and his brother to the sea, having a wife and child on shore, he is "no crusader after perils; for him courage was not a sentiment; but a thing simply useful to him, and always at hand upon all mortally practical occasions" (915). To Starbuck, whaling is a business, as it is to Peleg and Bildad; younger than they, he means to take risks only if he needs to take them in the course of getting the job done.

Why, then, does he serve Ahab? It is "not in reasonable nature," Ishmael acutely observes, "that a man so organized, and with such terrible experiences and remembrances as he had," not to have "engendered an element in him, which, under suitable circumstances, would break out from its confinement, and burn all his courage up" (915). Starbuck has physical courage, the virtue that stands between the vices of cowardice and rashness, but he "cannot withstand those more terrific, because more spiritual terrors, which sometimes menace you from the concentrating brow of an enraged and mighty man," an Ahab. Ishmael associates Starbuck's virtues with the nobility of human nature itself, and therefore with "democratic dignity," with "our divine equality" bestowed by the hand of "God," by which he means "the Spirit of Equality, which has spread one royal mantle of humanity over all my kind," raising men like John Bunyan, Cervantes, and Andrew Jackson from prison, pauperdom, and the common people (916). But Starbuck lacks the spiritual courage of Bunyan, the wit of Cervantes, and the vigor of Jackson.

Second mate Stubb displays a different sort of courage. "Good-humored, easy, and careless, he presided over his whale-boat as if the most deadly encounter were but a dinner, and his crew all invited guests." He lacks Starbuck's prudence. "What he thought of death itself, there is no telling. Whether he ever thought of it at all, might be a question." Later he will say that "Think not, is my eleventh commandment" (with "sleep when you can" being the twelfth); such thoughtlessness serves the tyrant's purposes although, unlike Ishmael, Stubb never needs to struggle to suppress thought. Nor does he much fear God, as his "almost impious good-humor" carries him along, cheerfully puffing his omnipresent pipe (918). Third mate Flask differs from both Stubb and Starbuck in being more thumotic; a lesser Ahab, he "somehow seemed to think that the great Leviathans had personally and hereditarily affronted him," and so he makes war against them, although without Ahab's grimness, or his grandness (919).

Each mate has a harpooneer serving under him on the hunt. Starbuck has Queequeg. Stubb has Tashtego, an Indian from Martha's Vineyard, a man descended from the original stock of Nantucket whalers. Flask has Ahasuerus Daggoo, a giant African who has "retained all his barbaric virtues." Ishmael observes that this division of labor, with the "native Americans" or white citizens ruling the non-white foreigners—the one group "provid[ing] the brains, the rest of the world as generously supplying the muscles"—reflects the American workforce generally (921). And like many Americans, the workers, too, are "isolatoes"—on the whaling ships generally so, as most of them are Islanders. America consists of isolatoes, albeit "federated along one keel," as the largely self-governing American states are federated (921). In this American vessel, there is one anomaly, a person who doesn't fit in to the purposes of the voyage. This is "black Little Pip," a "poor Alabama boy," whose only apparent function is to beat a tambourine (922). He is a mascot; he might be taken for an American slave, except that he does no useful work. In the end he will play the role of fool to Ahab's spiritually maddened tyrant/hero.

As the ship sails south, the warmth of the air finally brings the real ruler on deck. "His whole high, broad form, seemed made of solid bronze, and shaped in an unalterable mould, like Cellini's cast Perseus" (924). Bronze is the symbol of God's judgment of sin; Ahab will attempt to judge and punish the Judge. Cellini's sculpture depicts the hero holding the head of Medusa, whom he has slain. After killing Medusa, whose gaze turned men into stone, Perseus rescued the princess Andromeda from the sea-monster, Cetus; he disposes of a rival suitor by holding Medusa's head aloft, petrifying the man. Ahab would also slay the monster, but as a tyrant it is his own gaze that petrifies men, enabling him to rule them. He is marked (like Cain?) with a thin scar from head to toe, possibly inflicted "in an elemental strife at sea" or perhaps a birth-mark—the claims about it differ (924). No one disputes the cause of his other deformity, the leg-stump left over from, indeed, an elemental strife at sea, his fight with the White Whale. His gaze radiates "an infinity of firmest fortitude, a determinate, unsurrenderable willfulness, in [its] fixed and fearless, forward dedication" (925). This notwithstanding, "some considering touch of humanity was in him," as he avoided the quarter-deck when the sailors slept below so as not to disturb them with the rapping of his whalebone peg-leg on the planks.

Yet, on one occasion, when "the mood was on him too deep for re-gardings," he forgets; second mate Stubb emerges to ask deferentially if his captain might find a way to muffle the sound. Ahab calls him a dog, orders him back to the kennel; the offended Stubb protests, so Ahab calls him ten times a donkey, a mule, and an ass, whereupon the hapless subordinate re-treats to nurse his wound (928). To a man of the greatest *thumos*, to a tyrant, to Ahab, Stubb is an object of contempt. Stubb protests the interruption of his own and the crew's physical needs while Ahab rages inwardly against his enemy and plots against the White Whale, an animal, rightly rebuked and ruled by the man of more intense fire. While Ahab throws away his pipe, a thing "meant for sereneness," more fit for a Stubb than "a great lord of Leviathan," Stubb falls asleep and dreams (930).

Melville titles the dream-chapter "Queen Mab." Stubb dreams that Ahab kicked him with his ivory leg. An old merman appears, who comforts him by saying he was "kicked by a great man"—an honor, and one which will make a wise man of him, too, if he understands that trying to kick back against a great man is like kicking a pyramid (932). The man of less heart than stomach will appease his heart so. Resentment without revenge is as high as his heart carries him.

Queen Mab, the Celtic name for the Faerie Queen, appears in at least two works of English literature Melville likely read. In *Romeo and Juliet*, lovestruck Romeo begins to tell cynical Malvolio of a dream he had. Malvo-lio cuts him short with a mocking speech about dreams; Queen Mab sup-posedly brings them to us, but in cold fact they depict our own wishes; the lawyer dreams of fees, the warrior of battlefield glory, and so on. If Melville alludes to this speech, he considers Stubb's dream as the kind of wishful thinking that brings Ishmael and many others to submit themselves to the tyrant's rule.

Queen Mab also appears as one of the two main characters in Percy Bysshe Shelley's early narrative poem of that name. The story there has nothing to do with Stubb's dream, but much to do with the character of Ahab. The poem is a *paean* to antagonism for the God of the Bible, begin-ning with its epigraph from Voltaire, "*Écrasez l'infame!*" Queen Mab casts a spell on the corpse of a dead maiden raising her "Spirit." She brings her far above the world to show her the vastness of the cosmos: "He who rightly feels [the universe's] infinity and grandeur is in no danger of seduction from the falsehoods of religious systems, or of deifying the principle of the universe." Such mere systems are too limited to comprehend the true infinity. All religions, but especially "the childish mummeries of the Jews" and, worse still, Christianity, cause most or even all evils on earth, including war, tyranny, selfishness, money-getting commerce, and slavery. Religion "peoplest earth with demons, hell with men, and heaven with slaves!" However, in a Spinozist or perhaps Hegelian turn, Queen Mab assures the Spirit that the true God, "the universal Spirit," "the Spirit of Nature" with its "all-sufficing Power, Necessity," guides us toward a better world. What men call God is only the personification of the unknown; what we need to know is that all is power, including the human mind, which has no free-will, and therefore cannot sin. There is no such thing as justice, "neither good nor evil in the universe"; all is utility, and therefore we have no reason to feel hatred or contempt. There is no "creative Divinity," separate from His Creation, but "a pervading Spirit coeval with the universe."

Therefore, "Ahasuerus, rise!" Queen Mab commands. In the Old Testament, Ahasuerus is a king of Persia, traditionally considered an example of the fool by medieval rabbis. In medieval legend, Ahasuerus is one name for the doorman at Pontius Pilate's estate who supposedly taunted Jesus on the way to the Cross. Cursed to "rive the earth from pole to pole" (in Shelley's telling) the Wandering Jew will not rest until the Second Coming. For Shelley, Ahasuerus is a hero who says, "the tyrants invented cruel torments, but did not kill me." The Spirit asks the risen Ahasuerus, "Is there a God?" Yes, he replies: He is a God of malice, his Son "a parish demagogue" who brought not peace but a sword "on earth to satiate with the blood of truth and freedom his malignant soul." A fit subject for Milton's Satan, who would rather rule in Hell than serve in Heaven, Ahasuerus prefers "Hell's freedom to the servitude of heaven." In one of his extensive prose endnotes, Shelley claims that the real Jesus was a human reformer who died precisely because he was a reformer who threatened the religious and secular powers of the day.

Queen Mab describes an 'end of History' as the "paradise of peace" where "Reason and passion cease to combat." There, the disease of madness will be readily cured by the right diet. The Spirit returns to earth, reunited with her body in a Hegelian synthesis of the spiritual and the material, overcoming the fatal and false disjunction of these, enforced by religions.

Harpooneer Ahasuerus Daggoo has indeed riven the earth from pole to pole. More pertinently, Ahab, whose name's first three letters are identical, and who has wandered even longer, will be seen to strike against what he takes to be the malignity of Being symbolized by the White Whale. Sure enough, Ahab interrupts the conversation in which Stubb tells his dream to Flask, shouting, "Look sharp, all of ye! There are whales hereabouts! If ye see a white one, split your lungs for him!" It is Ahab's first command to the whole crew. Stubb fears Ahab's bloody-mindedness. "Ahab has that that's bloody on his mind" (932). But he tells Flask to keep mum (932). He won't cross the tyrant again. Does he thereby submit to reality, or only to the more comprehensive dream, and to the grander but fatal dreamer?

## Chapter Four
# THE NATURE OF CHAOS

If the waters of the oceans represent and to some degree embody the chaos surrounding and even underlying the apparent order of the land—if chaos is an ineluctable reality on earth—how can that chaos be thought? And what shall, *can* human beings do when given it, and as part of it?

In the eleven chapters beginning with "Cetology" and ending with "The Whiteness of the Whale," Ishmael presents several attempts to understand and to deal with this reality. "Cetology" comes immediately after the first mention of the White Whale by Ahab, although we recall that Ishmael alluds to it near the beginning of his yarn. With characteristic irony, Ishmael presents a taxonomy of whales, a "classification of the constituents of chaos," which he calls "indispensable to a thorough appreciative understanding of the more special leviathanic revelations and allusions of all sorts which are to follow" (933). Because the sperm whale inhabits the remote southern seas, and offers only glimpses of itself above the surface, the two best books on the sperm whale which attempt a "scientific description" of the species "necessarily" offer little information. But Ishmael brushes that aside: "Any human thing supposed to be complete must for that reason infallibly be faulty" (934–935); limited human beings weakly comprehend a vastness that changes constantly. This does not preclude some insights, however.

On the question of whether the whale is a mammal or a fish, Ishmael cheerfully chooses to rely on tradition, not Linnaeus, even while observing that the 'fish' has lungs, not gills, and warm blood. The real reason for calling the whale a fish is that it lives entirely in the water, the symbol of chaos; that is, Ishmael does indeed undertake a leviat*hanic* classification. To his mind, mammals, including humans, are at most "amphibious," like the walrus and perhaps the sailor. He defines the whale "*a spouting fish with a horizontal tail*" unlike all other fish, the vertically-tailed ones "familiar to landsmen." Ishmael then lists the various kinds of whales, playfully dividing them first according to their size and naming their sizes in the terms used for books: folio, octavo, duodecimo. The analogy is apt: Neither a book nor a classification system can really 'contain' the vast reality it attempts to describe. "God keep me from completing anything. This whole book is but a draught—nay, but the draught of a draught" (946). Yet there are insights along the way: Regarding the killer whale, Ishmael observes, "We are all killers, on land and sea; Bonaparte and sharks included" (943). Classifying the constituents of chaos does not tame them, even if it may give human beings a framework, however arbitrary, for making observations that tell.

From science, Ishmael returns to politics, this time not the formal politics of rank but the perhaps more powerful order of custom, which enables rank to endure. Returning to the origins of European whaling, Ishmael recalls that the regime of the old Dutch whaling ships consisted of the captain, who took charge of navigation and general management of the vessel, and the *Specksynder* ("Fat-cutter"), who governed whale-hunting. On American whalers, the harpooner is "an important officer on the boat," even to the point of commanding the ship's deck on night watches in whaling grounds. For that reason, "the grand maxim of the sea demands, that he should nominally live apart from the men before the mast, and be in some way distinguished from their professional superior, although always, by them, familiarly regarded as their social equal" (947). The regime of the whaling ship consists of equality in civil society but of rank in terms of custom—custom based on the character of one's role within the regime.

This notwithstanding, the manifest ruler of the *Pequod* was Ahab. Yet even he "was by no means unobservant of the paramount forms and usages of the sea," although "incidentally making use of them for other and more private ends than they were legitimately intended to subserve." In this, Ahab resembles a 'classical' tyrant along the lines of Xenophon's Hiero, not a 'modern' or 'ideological' tyrant along the lines of Lenin, Hitler, or Mao Zedong. And so he must do; given "the sultanism of his brain," his drive to found an "irresistible dictatorship" aboard the ship will fail if he relies on natural intelligence alone. "Be a man's intellectual superiority what it will, it can never assume the practical, available supremacy over other men, without the aid of some sort of external arts and entrenchments, always, in themselves, more or less paltry and base"—necessary

"political superstitions." (For the modern tyrant, by contrast, ideology pa-
rades as absolute scientific knowledge, usually of the 'laws of History,' and
thereby replaces these old superstitions with new ones.) Indeed, the need
for convention is one reason why "God's true princes of the Empire"—
natural *aristoi* like Bulkington—fail to ascend to the heights of command
under egalitarian social conditions. A dolt may rule an empire because
"the plebeian herds crouch abased before the tremendous centralization"
of authority seen in a mere crown. (947–948) Far from being a dolt, when
a man like Ahab takes the helm, who understands the use of custom or
convention, the people will obey.

Ishmael shows how this works by describing the ritual of dining at the
Captain's table. Each officer must, according to "holy usage," report to the
cabin after the higher-ranking officer has had time to be seated; all eat in
silence (952). ("Though nominally included in the census of Christendom,
[Ahab] was still alien in it," socially "inaccessible" even at table (955).)
When the officers leave, the harpooneers dine rather more informally, in
an "almost frantic democracy" of gobbling and chatter (953). But democracy establishes its own hierarchy; the men take their amusement by intim-
idating the cabin boy; "hard fares the white waiter who waits upon
cannibals" (954).

Formal office and informal usage or custom reinforce any regime. To
these rulers typically add architecture. Mast-heads embody authority, literally towering over the crew. Ishmael sketches a history of 'mast-heads,' de-
fined broadly as any elevated structure that either enables surveillance or
forces onlookers to bend their heads upward, beginning with the pyramids
of Egypt and including statues of George Washington and other dignitaries.
On the whaling ship, however, elevation often induces neither vigilance
nor awe but freedom from the captain's orders (how can he tell if you are
really looking out for a whale, or just daydreaming?) Although "very often
do the captains of such ships take those absent-minded young philosophers"—Rousseauians, no doubt, given to the reveries of the solitary
sailor—"to task, upbraiding them with feeling insufficient 'interest' in the
voyage," they remain out of reach, so "lulled into such an opium-like list-
lessness of vacant unconscious reverie" by "the blending cadence of waves
with thoughts, that at last he loses his identity; takes the mystic ocean at
his feet for the visible image of that deep, blue, bottomless soul, pervading

mankind and nature" (961). In a word, the young sentry finds not whales but pantheism, an insight falsified not so much by the captain's wrath, by the regime under which he serves, as by the *natural* fact that his perch is precarious: "Move your foot or hand an inch; slip your hold at all; and your identity comes back in horror," hovering as you do over "Descartesian vortices" through which you might fall into that "summer sea," no longer quite so mystical (962). Whatever one might think of monism and dualism in theory, in practice a duality of solid and airy substances pertains, with the sea-water underlying both. If the mast-head architecture lifts a sailor above the reach of the ship's rulers, the natural laws that govern both men and their artifacts refute any false speculations he may dream up.

Office, custom, and architecture may suffice for ruling a regime under ordinary circumstances, but how to rule such a motley crew of all races, of what Nietzsche would later call a cosmopolitan carnival of arts, worships, and moralities? And how to rule a whaling ship (or a regime like America's) for an extraordinary purpose, under harsh conditions? Ahab knows how. He commands the crew to gather on his quarter-deck and offers them a material inducement: "Whosoever of ye raises me that [...] white whale, he shall have this gold ounce, my boys!" (965) The sailors cheer, and Ahab breaks out the grog to celebrate their unity of purpose. But Starbuck demurs. Ahab is usurping the authority of the owners of the ship, staging a *coup d'etat* in their absence. "I came here to hunt whales," Starbuck protests, "not my commander's vengeance." To establish his tyranny beyond the supports of office, custom, and architecture, Ahab must put down this murmur of rebellion against his rebellion. If the purpose of whaling is to make money, I, Ahab, have just offered money, a doubloon reward: "My vengeance will fetch a great premium *here*!" The material rewards whaling offers the sailors are years distant and uncertain, a percentage of the profits at the end of the voyage. The doubloon is here and now. 'The people' incline to follow the nearer, more concrete payout.

His challenge blocked by this demagogic appeal to low-but-solid material motives, Starbuck invokes the other great incentive animating New England whalers. "Vengeance on a dumb brute! that simply smote thee from blindest instinct! Madness! To be enraged with a dumb thing, Captain Ahab, seems blasphemous!" (967) But Ahab has an answer to this spiritual challenge, too—a call not to spirituality but to spiritedness. "All visible objects, man, are but as pasteboard masks"—he begins as if he were Emerson, a Transcendentalist—but behind the brutish matter of this whale, the white whale, lurks "an inscrutable malice," not the supposedly benevolent nature Emersonians imagine. "That inscrutable thing is chiefly what I hate; and be the white whale agent, or be the white whale principal, I will wreak that hate upon him. Talk not to me of blasphemy, man; I'd strike the sun if it insulted me" (967). *Man*: Ahab calls Starbuck and the crew to manliness; if Shelley's Queen Mab reveals a universe supporting an anti-Biblical atheism of delight and freedom, Ahab reveals a universe supporting an anti-Biblical atheism of pure *thumos*. As for Ahasuerus' conviction that God is malicious, Ahab transfers that hatred to the Whale. Politically, he knows he has the crew, 'the people,' behind him, against Starbuck's sober but weaker spiritual and reasonable aristocratism. "The crew, man, the crew! Are they not one and all with Ahab, in this matter of the whale?" They are, and Ahab sees that "Starbuck now is mine; he cannot oppose me now, without rebellion" not simply against Ahab as a man but against Ahab as the tyrant whose rhetoric has overmatched Starbuck's pleading. The first mate is reduced to prayer: "God keep me!—keep us all!" Neither Ahab nor, as it will transpire, God 'hears,' heeds the prayer, but below deck the mysterious sailors whom Elijah asked about, the ones who have yet to come on deck, laugh in mocking delight. Ahab commands that the sailors on deck drink the grog ("It's hot as Satan's hoof"), an order they do not hesitate to obey. Parodying a Roman Catholic mass, Ahab authorizes his "three pagan kinsmen," the harpooneers, as his priests, who pass around "the murderous chalices" of grog. Pale, shuddering Starbuck turns away from the triumph of Milton's Satan, who has justified his ways to men and thereby fixed them to his regime of tyranny, by their own impassioned assent.

The literary-political scholar John Alvis has commented on Ahab's brilliant, sinister use of demagoguery to rule souls, not merely bodies.[7] The Apostle Peter understands demagogues well enough to describe men like Ahab. "There were false prophets [...] among the people" of Israel, Peter writes, and there will be "false teachers among you, who privately shall bring

---

7     John Alvis: "*Moby-Dick* and Melville's Quarrel with America." *Interpretation: A Journal of Political Philosophy*, Volume 23, Number 2, Winter 1996, pp. 223–247. Alvis remarks that Ahab never employs force, tyrant though he is.

in damnable heresies, even denying the Lord that bought them, and bring upon themselves swift destruction." Coming from within Christendom itself, they will appeal to you with covetousness, while "with feigned words mak[ing] merchandise out of you"; your greed for gain will turn to their profit. They will "despise government," as Ahab despises the government of the ship's owners; "self-willed, they are not afraid to speak evil of dignities." They will "count it a pleasure to riot in the day time," or at least pass around the grog for others to do so. And so they "beguile unstable souls," with "great swelling words of vanity." Having described men like Ahab, Peter writes what might be called a verse for Starbuck: "Of whom a man is overcome, of the same is he brought in bondage" (2 Peter 2). Does anyone on the *Pequod* think of Peter? Ishmael turns to the thoughts of captain, officers, and crew in the next four, brief chapters.

If Ahab is right about Being, those whom Peter calls false prophets are the true ones, including Ahab himself. His day's work done, the Captain, alone in his cabin, gazes out the windows at the sunset. He reflects on the crown he has successfully usurped; the metal in it is iron, not gold. The "dry heat" of the sunset no longer soothes his soul, as it once did. "This lovely light, it lights not me; all loveliness is anguish to me, since I can ne'er enjoy. Gifted with high perception"—insight into the malignity of Being—"I lack the low enjoying power" of his officers and crew. "Damned, most subtly and most malignantly! damned in the midst of Paradise!" Ahab is Adam, but an Adam not humbled by God or comforted by God's creation, allied with the serpent. His will is iron, like the substance of the doubloon; that is his true crown: "What I've dared, I've willed; and what I've willed I'll do!" Soft Starbuck thinks him mad, but Ahab knows himself better, as worse: "I'm demoniac, I am madness maddened!" "I now prophesy that I will dismember my dismemberer," become "the prophet and the fulfiller" all in one, guaranteeing his prophecy by his own action (971). He would thereby rival God, the only one who can fully unify plan and action. *His* regime, his way of life, shall be "the iron way." But will he be a true or a false prophet?

A little later, at dusk, Starbuck leans on the mainmast, nursing his injuries. "My soul is more than matched; she's"—note the feminine form—"overmanned; and by a madman!" Starbuck's "sanity" has failed, and not only politically but morally: "He drilled down deep, and blasted all my reason out of me!" Ahab "would be a democrat to all above," challenging God, but "look, how he lords it over all below!" Starbuck's "miserable office" will be "to obey, rebelling," and "worse yet, to hate with a touch of pity," since "in his eyes I read some lurid woe would shrivel me up, had I it." Starbuck can only take refuge in wishful thinking. "His heaven-insulting purpose, God may wedge aside" (973). Or not, God having his own purposes, His thoughts not being ours. Ahab has revealed something to Starbuck: "Oh, life! 'tis now that I do feel the latent horror in thee!" Gathering himself, he adds, "but 'tis not me! that horror's out of me! and with the soft feeling of the human in me, yet will I try to fight ye, ye grim, phantom figures!" He prays to the "blessed influences" for help in this (973–974). But will those influences answer his prayer?

Still later, on the night watch, Stubb has "been thinking over it ever since, and that ha-ha's the final consequence"—the 'H' sound of awe, filtered through his comic-shallow soul. "A laugh's the wisest, easiest answer to all that's queer." The unthoughtful man makes a suitably thoughtless prophecy: "I know not all that may be coming, but be it what it will, I'll go to it laughing" (975).

Latest of all, the harpooneers and sailors sing drunkenly, to the time of Pip's tambourine. The old Manx sailor prophesies to himself, "I wonder whether these jolly lads bethink them of what they are dancing over. I'll dance over your grave, I will [...]" (978). (In fact, he will not.) As a storm comes up, Daggoo and a Spaniard exchange racial slurs and start to fight; Tashtego observes, "gods and men—both brawlers!" while the much-insulted slave boy Pip says to himself, "that anaconda of an old man swore 'em to hunt" Moby-Dick—white men, white whale, white squall blowing, and the "big white God aloft," to whom he prays for mercy (981–982).

In the regime of isolatoes, only drunken sailors socialize, but their revelry ends in a fight. Ishmael pauses his yarn to make his confession: "I, Ishmael, was one of that crew; my shouts had gone up with the rest; my oath had been welded with theirs; and stronger I shouted, and more did I hammer and clinch my oath, because of the dread in my soul" (983). Human encounters with the White Whale had proven not only injurious but "fatal to the last degree of fatalities" (984); according to both Job and Hobbes, death is the king of terrors. Such terror generates legends that deepen the terror. Moby-Dick is ubiquitous, having been "encountered in opposites latitudes at one and the same instant of time"; Moby-Dick is immortal ("for immortality is but ubiquity in time"). "But even stripped of these supernatural surmisings," which make Moby-Dick into a god, or perhaps an angel of death, "there was enough in the earthly and incontestable character of the monster to strike the imagination with unwonted power"—namely, his "snow-white wrinkled forehead"; his "high, pyramidical [mast-head-like] white hump"; and his body, streaked, spotted, marbled with white (987). Above all, Moby-Dick inspires "natural terror" by his actions, the "unexampled intelligent malignity" with which he would retreat from pursuing whale boats, only to turn on them and destroy them with an "infernal foresight of ferocity" (988). Far from the dumb brute of Starbuck's description, Moby-Dick acts like a brilliant military captain and assault force, combined.

This is why Ahab hates him. Commanding a whale ship, Ahab had descended onto one of the pursuit boats; Moby-Dick smashed all three boats, and Ahab bravely continued his assault, stabbing the monster. "Moby-Dick had reaped away Ahab's leg, as a mower a blade of grass in the field. No turbaned Turk, no hired Venetian or Malay, could have smote him with more seeming malice." Ahab came to load "all his intellectual and spiritual exasperations" on the White Whale, now "the monomaniac incarnation of all those malicious agencies which some deep men feel eating in them" (988–989). Unlike the devil-worshippers of the ancient East, Ahab did not worship the evil one but "piled on the whale's white hump the sum of all the general rage and hate felt by his whole race from Adam down." In his delirium on the voyage home, "his torn body and gashed soul bled into one another; and so interfusing, made him mad" (989). By the time he reached Nantucket, however, he had learned to conceal that madness. His "great natural intellect," entirely preserved, now served not as the ruler of his passion but as its "living instrument," with intellect and madness binding to gather in his soul "a thousand fold more potency than ever he had sanely brought to bear upon any one reasonable object" (990). The man who would strike through the mask of appearance to the evil underlying all Being mimics the prey he hunts, and sane Nantucketers like Mr. Peleg fell for the ruse.

Indeed, they thought, wishfully, that Ahab's war against the White Whale will make him "superlatively competent to cheer and howl on his underlings to the attack," lending energy to the purpose of their intended commercial regime on the whaling ship. "Had any of his old acquaintances on shore but half dreamed of what was lurking in him then, how soon would their aghast and righteous souls have wrenched the ship from such a fiendish man! They were bent on profitable cruises, the profit to be counted down in dollars from the mint. He was intent on an audacious, immitigable, and supernatural revenge." Peleg called him an "ungodly, godly man"; he got it half right, as Ishmael now accurately calls him an "ungodly old man" at "the head of a crew [...] chiefly made up of mongrel renegades, and castaways, and cannibals—morally enfeebled also, by the incompetence of mere unaided virtue or right-mindedness in Starbuck, the invulnerable jollity of indifference and recklessness in Stubb, and the pervading mediocrity of Flask" (992). And there is more than that. The officers and crew unite under Ahab's tyrannical regime because there is something of him in each human being. "The subterranean miner works in us all." So, "for one, I gave myself up to abandonment of the time and the place; but while yet all a-rush to encounter the whale, could see naught in that brute but the deadliest of ill" (992). No Christian, Ishmael nonetheless discovers what Augustine discovered in himself, that he would do evil while knowing it evil. In this, both men achieve self-knowledge while learning what human nature is. Socrates considers this the dual purpose of philosophy.

This being the nature of man, what is the nature of the Whale, and especially the nature of his whiteness? From the "classification of the constituents of chaos" in Chapter 32 Ishmael arrives at "the whiteness of the whale" in Chapter 42—whiteness, which has no constituents. Ahab defines the Whale by his malice. Ishmael defines him by his whiteness.

"It was the whiteness of the whale that above all things appalled me" (993). But why? Is whiteness not an emblem of the Good? Ishmael not only acknowledges that it is often taken to be such, he offers examples of the thought from many regimes and civilizations ranging from European empires: ancient (Rome) and modern (Austria), both western, to the monarchy of Siam (modern) and the "Persian fire-worshippers" (ancient), both eastern. Does not the Book of Revelation itself envision the "white robes of the redeemed," the "great white throne" of God? (994) On land, the White Steed of the Prairies recorded in Indian traditions "always to the bravest Indians [...] was the object of trembling reverence and awe" (996).

At sea, the albatross has proved a somewhat more ambiguous presence, a creature of "spiritual wonderment and pale dread." "Not Coleridge first threw that spell; but God's great, unflattering laureate, Nature" (995). Whiteness has another dimension to it. "Witness the white bear of the poles, and the white shark of the tropics; what but their smooth, flaky whiteness makes them the transcendent horrors they are?" (994) An albino human being unsettles us. As do the living who pale at the sight of such beings, as do the dead, who wear their "pallor" as "the badge of consternation in the other world" (997). In the Bible, Death is personified as the pale rider on the pale horse, king of terrors both in the Christian Book of Revelation and the *Leviathan* of the materialist Hobbes. "Therefore, in his other moods, symbolize whatever grand or gracious thing he will by whiteness, no man can deny that in its profoundest idealized significance it calls up a peculiar apparition to the soul," in reversal of the benign Transcendentalism of Melville's contemporaries. "To analyze it, would seem impossible," as whiteness has no parts (997). In recalling Pip's thought about white men, white whale, white squall, white God, one sees the whiteness marbled into everyone, everything.

But is our understanding of whiteness only a matter of our "moods"? Is our sometime terror at it nothing but sickly fear? No: Tell me, Ishmael challenges his reader, why a strong, young colt, "foaled in some peaceful valley in Vermont," will panic at the smell of a buffalo robe. The colt has never been gored by a bison, an animal which departed from that land decades or centuries ago. "Here thou beholdest even in a dumb brute"—a creature that is what Starbuck wrongly supposes Moby-Dick to be—"the instinct of the knowledge of the demonism in the world." "Though in many of its aspects this visible world seems formed in love, the invisible spheres were formed in fright" (1000). This means that not only does Ishmael reject the God of the Bible, as Ahab does, not only does he reject Emerson's vision of a nature whose "aspect is devout," but he comes nearer to Ahab's claim about the underlying nature of Nature. He presents his readers with a choice. Given whiteness's "indefiniteness," by which it "shadows forth the heartless voids and immensities of the universe," one might recall Pascal, terrified by those voids and immensities (1001). The whiteness "shadows," the whiteness darkens souls with fear. For Pascal, that fear was, as the Bible wants it to be for us, the beginning of wisdom—the fear of God. But is there a God? Here is the second choice: "Is it, that as in essence whiteness is not so much a color as the visible absence of color, and at the same time the concrete of all colors; is it for these reasons that there is such a dumb blankness, full of meaning, in a wide landscape of snows—a colorless, all-color of atheism from which we shrink?" (1002) Does the faith that may issue from our fear of God only amount to a comforting cover for our greater fear that there is no God? That the careful separations established by the Creator-God of the Bible amount only to illusions, poor attempts to put limits on the all-encompassing whiteness of Being?

Leaving theology aside, the "natural philosophers" have discovered "that all the other earthly hues—every stately or lovely emblazoning—the sweet tinges of sunset skies and woods; yea, and the gilded velvets of butterflies, and the butterfly cheeks of young girls; all these are but subtle deceits, not actually inherent in substances, but only laid on from without; so that all deified Nature absolutely paints the harlot, whose allurements cover nothing but the charnel-house within." Let there be light, the God of Genesis commands, but "the great principle of light, for ever remains white or colorless in itself"; to consider it truly we must realistically see that "the palsied universe lies before us a leper," its whiteness a horrifying and fatal disease. "And of all these things the Albino whale was the symbol. Wonder ye then at the fiery hunt?" Why would men, "deep men," men who see truly, not want to destroy their would-be destroyer, before it can destroy them? (1001) For Ahab, and evidently for Ishmael, no faerie queen, no Mab, will redeem us with some brighter tomorrow. In *Moby-Dick* Melville not only anticipates the 'spiritual' tyrants of the next century but rejects their cheery illusions of utopia, with which they would beguile the vast crews under the sway of their regimes.

Although Ishmael explains Ahab's whale-hunt, he does not thereby endorse its purpose, or Ahab's regime. In dispelling the wonder at whalers and whaling, Ishmael shows why all human beings prove vulnerable to Ahabian appeals, to the demagoguery that induces them to assent to the madness of the tyrant, the tyranny of madness. We all have in us what Ahab has in him. To show what we have in us is not to commend it. Ishmael succumbed, but has broken the spell. He would not have "Young America" under the spell of a tyrant any more than he would have it under the influence of the grog of bullying, brawling democracy. Neither nature as understood by the

American Founders, from which right may be derived, nor the nature of Emerson or the nature of Shelley, beckoning us to utopian illusions, nor the nature of Ahab, cunningly malignant and thus justifying tyranny, adequately comprehends nature. Nothing adequately *comprehends* it, if comprehension means an all-encompassing, systematic understanding, parodied in "Cetology." If the universe is diseased, it cannot be the foundation of right or of utopia; nor is it properly the object of rage, inasmuch as disease bespeaks no malice. Disease does not bespeak anything; it is dumb. A calmer state of mind, properly fearful but not paralyzed with fear, will be needed in the New American and in the soul of the New American.

## Chapter Five
# LIVING WITH CHAOS

If the palsied universe lies before us like a leper, what shall we do? What way of life, what regime, should human beings follow?

Democracy would be one possibility. The principle of democracy is equality, and if we are all equally illumined not by the light of the Gospels, nor that of the Enlightenment, but by the colorless all-color of atheism, no one, no few, among us deserves to rule the others. Such pretensions belong among the pretensions Nature paints, in painting herself like a harlot. Nor should democrats be dismissed as entirely ignorant. They hear things. If they are beneath some in civil society, this does keep their ears to the ground, or in this case to the deck. A sailor believes he's heard something below the deck of the *Pequod*, something or someone not yet seen on deck. He does not know what or who it is, and the crew both discounts his opinion and passes it around. (Readers know he heard the mysterious stowaways; Melville titles the chapter "Hark!" but the herald angels aren't singing.) Low to the social ground, democrats hear things, even if they might not immediately know what they are. Ishmael never suggests that the officers have heard anything below-deck. Superior rank makes rule easier in one way, harder in another.

Tyranny is another possible way of life, represented by Ahab. Ishmael shows him poring over his sea charts, calculating where Moby-Dick might most likely be found, given the known, regular migrations of sperm whales—their 'fatedness.' This instances the way in which Ahab's intellect serves his ruling passion, "threading the maze of currents and eddies, with a view to the more certain accomplishment of the monomaniac thought of his soul," forming a "delirious but still methodical scheme" (1003). In the meantime (and here chance might intervene amidst the workings of fatality and human will), Moby-Dick may turn up anywhere, long before the ship reaches the most likely hunting ground; Ahab will keep the crew vigilant. As for himself, he remains superficially rational but tormented, awakening from fitful sleep with "his own bloody nails in his palms," self-crucified. The "hell in himself" drives him from his state room to pace every part of the deck. The "eternal, living principle of soul in him," his heart, in a state of "horror" at the underlying 'nature of nature,' conflicts with his mind, whose "sheer inveteracy of will" drives him to confront and attempt to destroy that nature. More, his heart is "horror-stricken" by the very mind that sets his purpose. His "tormented spirit" may be "a ray of living light, to be sure, but without an object to color, and therefore a blankness in itself," a miniature of the Leviathan he seeks to destroy. "God help thee, old man, thy thoughts have created a creature in thee; and he whose intense thinking thus makes him a Prometheus; a vulture feeds upon that heart for ever; that vulture the very creature he creates" (1007–1008). Rarely does skeptical Ishmael go so far as to appeal to God, but he sees the whiteness of the whale, a "blankness," in the soul of his captain, and doubts that any human word or deed can help him, or the regime he has founded (1008). Ahab's tyranny is *contra natura* in two ways: It takes the underlying whiteness of nature to be malicious instead of indifferent; and it tears at the life-principle in his own soul while causing the men under his command to sail to their deaths.

Ishmael admits that Ahab does understand *something* about nature. In another of his 'down-to-earth' chapters, he testifies to the fact that Moby-Dick, if a prodigy, nonetheless has had predecessors for elusiveness and ferocity among the sperm whale species. Ishmael protests that his yarn is no "monstrous fable, or worse and more detestable, a hideous and intolerable allegory" (1011). Sperm whales have indeed attacked whaling boats and ships, but land-dwellers seldom hear of these incidents and have little comprehension of the "powerful, knowing, and judiciously malicious" character of the monster, which "acts not so often with blind rage, as with willful, deliberate designs of destruction to his pursuers," behavior attested to as early as the sixth-century historian Procopius of Constantinople (1012). Wise Solomon was right: "Verily there is nothing new under the sun." Deploying understatement to drive home the plausibility of what he reports, Ishmael writes, "I tell you, the sperm whale will stand no nonsense" (1014).

His own credibility (and not incidentally, his own sanity) confirmed, Ishmael returns to the mind of the tyrant, whose rationality of method entails not only calculations concerning the Whale but ruling calculations concerning his officers and crew. "To accomplish his object Ahab must use tools; and of all tools used in the shadow of the moon, men are most apt to get out of order" (1018). Although for the moment Ahab has lodged "his magnet in Starbuck's brain," he knows that the soul of his First Mate "abhorred his captain's quest," and might challenge is rule; the conflict between mind and life-principle or soul which torments Ahab also torments Starbuck, thanks to Ahab. But in Starbuck this mindset was not self-generated, and so might slip out of Ahab's control. What's more, the length of the voyage might serve to detach the souls of his crew from his regime. He has brought them to a high pitch of excitement and resolution with his demagoguery, but he knows that this mood cannot endure through long months at sea. More, "he had indirectly laid himself open to the unanswerable charge of usurpation," giving his officers and crew a right to revolution, should they so choose (1020). "The subtle insanity of Ahab respecting Moby-Dick was noways more significantly manifested than in his superlative sense and shrewdness in foreseeing that, for the present, the hunt should in some way be stripped of that strange imaginative impiousness which naturally invested in it; that the full terror of the voyage must be kept withdrawn into the obscure background (for few men's courage is proof against protracted meditation unrelieved by action)" (1019). Therefore, action they will have, "some nearer things to think of than Moby-Dick," "some food for their common, daily appetites"—namely, cash. Even the doubloon will not suffice, here, but rather the continuance of "the natural, nominal purpose of the *Pequod's* voyage"—whale-hunting and whale-processing for salable commodities (1019).

The lull before action affords Ishmael an opportunity further to picture his own understanding of the human condition. On deck on the ship in a quiet sea, he and Queequeg weave a sword-mat, a sturdy cloth designed to protect sails and riggings at the chafing points against the masts. "It seemed as if this were the Loom of Time, and I myself were a shuttle mechanically weaving and weaving away at the Fates." The warp (the set of vertical threads, called the "longitude" by weavers) represents necessity or fate; "with my own hand I ply my own shuttle and weave my own destiny into these unalterable threads"—free will and liberty of action. "Meantime, Queequeg's impulsive, indifferent sword"—the piece of wood so called, which

opens a space in the woof (the horizontal threads or "latitude" of the mat)—
"sometimes hitting the woof slantingly, or crookedly, or strongly, or weakly,"
represents chance. Longitude and latitude: They are terms not only of weaving but preeminently of mapping; Ishmael and Queequeg's actions parallel
Ahab's. Their purpose contrasts with his, as protection contrasts with destruction. Maps picture parts of the earth; nature itself consists of warp and
woof, longitude and latitude, structures in which human choice may intervene—weaving itself into th favbric, even if it cannot create the fabric.
Against Shelley's thoroughgoing determinism in "Queen Mab," Ishmael as-
serts a limited but still significant role for free will and chance in the workings of fate. Despite his earlier appeal to God, Ishmael leaves no apparent
role for providence.

Chance intervenes. Tashtego sights a school of sperm whales. At this,
Ahab is "surrounded by five dusky phantoms that seemed fresh formed out
of air," rather like demons in the Bible (1023). These are those whom Ishmael had seen in the dusk, as he walked to board the ship in Nantucket,
the ones the sailor heard below deck. They unhitch a fourth whale boat,
which the sailors had assumed to be only a spare; Ahab himself will join
the hunt with these confederates. The dominant one, Fedallah, whose name
means "in the hands of God," or perhaps "gift of God," speaks in a serpentine half-hiss; tall, dark-skinned, garbed in black, his head is crowned with
the whiteness associated with the whale—long, white hair braided and
curled atop his head like a turban. He is a Parsee—that is, a Zoroastrian
fire-worshipper whose race once lived in Persia before being driven to India
by Muslim persecutors who did not regard Zoroastrians as gifts from God.
The Satan-figure's confreres are Manilans of "tiger-yellow" complexions;
Ishmael calls the Filipinos of Manila "a race notorious for a certain dia-
bolism of subtlety," whom "some honest white mariners supposed to be the
paid spies and secret confidential agents on the water of the devil" (1024).
While by his irony Ishmael distances himself from such superstition, he
does not distance himself from the symbolic significance of Ahab's chosen
close collaborators—a sort of substitute set of officers he has placed at the
heart of his usurping regime, a decidedly shadowy shadow cabinet.

The ship's formal officers react in accordance with their several characters. Devil-may-care Stubb shouts to his men, "Never mind the brim-
stone—devils are good fellows enough"; he urges on his rowers with talk

of riches in "a tone […] strangely compounded of fun and fury" (1025). Starbuck finds relief in the whale-sighting: "This at least is duty; duty and profit hand in hand!" (1026) Flask gets up on Daggoo's shoulders for a better look at the prey; "the bearer looked nobler than the rider," as if "Passion and Vanity [were] stamping the living magnanimous earth," to little effect (1029). During the pursuit, Stubb is cheerful, Starbuck quiet, Flask voluble. As for Ahab, he addresses his boat-crew with "words best omitted here; for you live under the blessed light of the evangelical land." All set off amidst "the vast swells of the omnipotent sea," soon roiled by a squall (1031).

In Starbuck's boat, Ishmael witnesses the interplay of chance, fate, and choice the sword-mat symbolized. Starbuck orders Queequeg to throw the harpoon (ruling choice, chosen obedience), but a wind-swelled wave (chance) jostles the boat, causing the harpoon to miss its target. The storm (fate) intensifies; they lose sight of the other boats and of the ship. Hoping for rescue, Starbuck lights a lantern, which Queequeg holds. "There, then, he sat, holding up that imbecile candle in the heart of that almighty forlornness. There, then, he sat, the sign and symbol of a man without a faith, hopelessly holding up hope in the midst of despair" (1033). They don't find the ship until the fatality of natural necessity brings the dawn.

Melville titles the next chapter of Ishmael's yarn "The Hyena"—a jarring title in a maritime narrative. "There are certain queer times and occasions in this strange mixed affair we call life when a man takes this whole universe for a vast practical joke," one "at nobody's expense but his own." "There is nothing like the perils of whaling to breed this free and easy sort of genial, desperado philosophy"—a sort of thoughtful Stubbism (1035). Safely back on ship, Ishmael asks Queequeg whether such near-calamities "did often happen," and is calmly assured that they do. He asks Starbuck if lowering whale boats in "a foggy squall is the height of the whaleman's discretion"; yes, "careful and prudent" Starbuck answers, having "lowered for whales from a leaking ship in a gale off Cape Horn." And you, Flask? "Yes, that's the law." (1035–1036) Constrained by fate, chance, and custom, Ishmael nonetheless has a choice to make, and so he does. He draws up his last will and testament, with Queequeg serving as "lawyer, executor, and legatee." And he feels better for doing so; as he says, "a stone was rolled away from my heart." He concludes that "the hyena" is life itself, the cosmos itself, a "laughing hyena"—a jolly beast, but ready to tear you apart (1036).

The best an individual can do is to make prudent choices against necessity and mischance, with the help of a trusted friend. Ishmael thus avoids the maddened *libido dominandi* of the tyrant's soul, the decent but weak conventionality of Starbuck, the thoughtless bravado of Stubb, the inanity of Flask, and what he judges to be the evangelical Christian hope of landlubbers who ignore the harshness of reality.

He remains under the rule of Ahab, where his modest morality will do only a little good. In one of his cheerier moments, Stubb marvels to Flask about peg-legged Ahab's courage at setting off in a whale-boat. "Oh! he's a wonderful old man!" Never one to miss a chance to exhibit stupidity, Flask observes that it's not "so strange," really, because Ahab has "one knee, a good part of the other left." Stubb ripostes: "I don't know that, my little man; I never saw him kneel" (1038). Surely not. Ishmael, who doesn't pray much, either, instead considers Ahab's political responsibility: Should the ship's captain risk his own life? The fact that he does, and the fact that he has engaged his own whale-boat crew, "never entered the heads of the owners of the *Pequod*," nor does it much trouble many of its officers or its sailors (1039).

As for Ahab's chosen crew-mates, Fedallah "remained a muffled mystery to the last," with "some sort of half-hinted influence" or "even authority" over the captain. Fedallah "was such a creature as civilized, domestic people in the temperate zone see only in their dreams," "the like of whom now and then glide among the unchanging Asiatic communities"—"insulated, immemorial, unalterable countries, which even in these modern days still preserve much of the ghostly aboriginalness of earth's primal recollections," memories of a time when "according to Genesis, the angels indeed consorted with the daughters of men," and "the devils also, add the uncanonical Rabbins, indulged in mundane amours" (1040). If lands untouched by civilization, or by modern notions of progress, no longer produce such remarkable men, the original earth, still preserved in some remote places, brings for 'Rousseuian' noble savages like Daggoo, Queequeg, and Tashtego, but also sinister beings like Fedallah, whom Rousseau would have dismissed as radically unnatural and therefore unlikely to exist in uncivilized places. Melville is a Rousseau for realists.

Such persons thrive on the chaos of the sea. It was primitive men (Tashtego's ancestors) who first ventured out on it to hunt whales. Fedallah is the first to see the Spirit-Spout, a will-o'-the-wisp whale-spout that vanishes when whaling boats chase it. "And had you watched Ahab's face that night, you would have thought in him [...] two different things were warring," his live leg and his dead, peg-leg. "On life and death this old man walked." "There reigned [...] a sense of peculiar dread at this flitting apparition, as if it were treacherously beckoning us on and on, in order that the monster might round on us, and rend us at last in the remotest and most savage seas" (1042). Savage persons on the savage sea: the more-or-less civilized sailors, split-souled Ahab included, associate the Spirit-Spout with Moby-Dick. They reach the Cape of Good Hope, which Ishmael, lost to hope, calls Cape Tomentosa, for its "demoniac waves." There they have their first encounter with another whale ship, "The Albatross," as white as its namesake, "long absent from home" (1045). Ahab tries to hail it, hoping for news of the Whale, but it drifts off, birdlike. In Coleridge's "Rime of the Ancient Mariner," the albatross is the bird of good omen. Ahab doesn't kill it, as the Mariner does; for him and his crew, it is simply unreachable.

Ahab commands the helmsman to sail on, "round the world." Ishmael reflects: "Round the world! There is much in that sound to inspire proud feelings; but whereto does all that circumnavigation conduct? Only through numberless perils to the very point whence we started, where those that we left behind secure, were all the time before us." If the world were "an endless plain," at least there *could* be progress, "promise in the voyage." "But in pursuit of those far mysteries we dream of, or in tormented chase of that demon phantom that, some time or other, swims before all human hearts; while chasing such over this round globe, they either lead us on in barren mazes or midway leave us whelmed" (1046). Given the futility of progress on a globe, where should the ship of state sail? Should it sail at all, or only keep to port?

*Chapter Six*

# REVOLUTION

"Isolatoes" may populate this novel, but social and political relations persist. The "gam"—a social meeting between two or more whale-ships at sea— endures as a tradition no other type of ocean-going ship upholds. Typically, sailors on the outward-bound ship give letters to the homeward-bound ship for delivery to families and sweethearts in Nantucket; in exchange, the homeward-bound sailors offer information on whales they've seen on their voyage. It is almost needless to say that Ahab has no use for such social exchanges, unless the other captain has seen Moby-Dick. But such single-minded and unsocial behavior can exact a political price.

"The Town-Ho's Story" is the longest chapter of the book. A yarn within the yarn, it consists of a story Ishmael tells to a pair of "Spanish friends" at the Golden Inn in Lima, Peru, some time after the voyage of the *Pequod*.[8] A whale-ship out of Nantucket, manned mostly by Polynesians, the *Town-Ho*'s name derives from another whaling tradition: Before whalemen shouted "There she blows" upon sighting a whale, they shouted "Town-ho." "Town" is an Indian word, originally signifying that the speaker has seen a whale twice—a confirmed sighting. In English it originally referred to a closed-in garden, and eventually to a small, urbanized community as distinguished from a village and from the countryside. All of these threads work into the yarn. As for "Ho," it's another 'H'-expulsion of breath, as is the word for the monster whose presence it signifies.

Ahab does want to talk with the captain of this ship because the crew has encountered Moby-Dick. But there was "a secret part of the tragedy"

---

8    Readers of Melville's later novella, *Billy Budd*, will recognize in the characters Steelkilt and Radney certain parallels between Billy Budd and First Mate Claggart. The circumstances and the actions narrated also 'rhyme,' if not exactly. Melville has spun Ishmael's yarn in a similar but not identical direction, tracing somewhat different dimensions of political life.

that Ahab and his officers never learn, a party "which seemed obscurely to involve with the whale a certain wondrous, inverted visitation of one of those so called judgments of God which at times are said to overtake some men" (1052). Tyrants and oligarchs alike isolate themselves from their subjects, even as they rule them. As a result, they fail to learn some things. They often attempt to overcome this handicap by forming a network of spies—secrecy against secrecy. Ahab and the officers seem not to have taken this precaution.

Cruising the Pacific Ocean, the *Town-Ho* had developed a slow leak, which its crew attributed fancifully or playfully to a swordfish. There was no real emergency, as the pumps kept the ship afloat. Most captains stay at sea under these conditions, as long as they are fairly close to land. Only when they are far out at sea does a captain worry, setting sail for some harbor. The choice is thus a matter of prudential judgment made within the constraints of geographic location and the condition of the ship. A few decades later, when thinking about 'ships of state,' scholars would begin to call such matters 'geopolitics.' Such judgments are what rulers are expected to make; to question their judgment is to question their authority to rule, to threaten revolution, regime change—mutiny.

On the *Town-Ho*, regime conflict arose from a small thing, a private conflict between Steelkilt, a "desperado" from Buffalo, New York, a "Lakeman"—a man who sailed the Great Lakes before signing on to the whaleship—and Radney, the first mate, a sharp-edged Nantucketer (1054). Ishmael explains to Pedro and Sebastian that the Great Lakes are "grand fresh-water seas," having "many of the ocean's noblest trait; with many of its rimmed varieties of races and climes." These include "two great contrasting nations"—sharply contrasting indeed, as in the 1850s veterans of the War of 1812 still lived who remembered naval battles on those seas. On shore there are still military batteries, "wild barbarians," and beasts of prey; on the seas, shipwrecks occur every year. "Thus, gentleman, though an inlander, Steelkilt was wild-ocean born, and wild-ocean nurtured." For his part, though a townsman and not a lakeman, Radney "was quite as vengeful and full of social quarrel as the backwoods seaman, fresh from the latitudes of buck-horn handled Bowie-knives." Just as Radney has "some good-hearted traits," to go with his asperities, so Steelkilt "had long been retained harmless and docile," and might have remained so, if treated with "inflexible firmness, only tempered by that common decency of human recognition which is the meanest slave's right." But Radney proved a poor ruler, "doomed and mad" (1055). In this, he resembles Ahab, albeit with neither the intelligence nor the megalomania. Radney was a tyrant, but a petty tyrant.

Somewhat concerned by the leak, Radney ordered the sails hoisted to speed the journey to the ship's "island haven" (1058). Because he was no coward, the sailors suspected his worry arose because he was a part-owner of the ship; so they joked, amongst themselves. The choice to change the ship's course belongs to the captain; presumably, Radney persuaded him. But Radney had a problem in ruling, not with the captain or the sailors but with one sailor in particular. "As you well know," Ishmael tells his friends, "it is not seldom the case in this conventional world of ours—watery or otherwise; that when a person placed in command over his fellowmen finds one of them to be very significantly his superior in general pride of manhood, straightway against that man he conceives an unconquerable dislike and bitterness; and he have a chance he will pull down and pulverize that subaltern's tower, and make a little heap of dust out of it" (1056). So Radney regarded Steelkilt, that "tall and noble animal with a head like a Roman" and "a brain, and a heart, and a soul in him […] which had made Steelkilt Charlemagne, had he been born son to Charlemagne's father" (1056). Nature made Steelkilt a king, indeed an emperor, king of kings; chance and convention had made him a subject, a sailor. By nature but not by convention, a Steelkilt should rule a Radney (a man "ugly as a mule; yet as hardy, as malicious") (1056). Rule by convention is both necessary—a means of ruling the unruly—and at times unnatural, unjust, at least to the extent that justice may be said to retain some foothold in a nature chaotic as the sea. Rule by convention is necessary because, as an earlier chapter taught us, many human beings will not obey rulers consistently without the habituation custom induces. The natural ruler who challenges conventional rule threatens the necessary conditions of *any* rule within a real, non-utopian human community. America's Declaration of Independence, its founding revolutionary statement, acknowledges this: "Prudence, indeed, will dictate that Governments long established should not be changed for light and transient causes; and accordingly all experience hath shewn, that mankind are more disposed to suffer, while evils are sufferable, than to right themselves by abolishing the forms to which they are accustomed."

Given this morally compromised, politically tense, and emotionally grating circumstance, Radney "did not love Steelkilt, and Steelkilt knew it" (1056). Steelkilt did enjoy a small measure of conventional authority as the leader of the pump gang which keeps the ship afloat. Seeing Radney draw near while they worked, he pretended not to notice him, bantering with his mates about Radney's "investment," his "estate" in the ship and his supposed over-caution motivated by that self-interest (1057). For his part, Radney pretended not to hear the chatter; taking refuge in his conventional right to command, he angrily ordered the men to pump harder. They did. Radney then foolishly pressed his advantage. When the crew took a rest break, he ordered the exhausted Steelkilt to sweep the deck, a menial task for boys; "plainly [he] meant to sting and insult Steelkilt, as though Radney had spat in his face" (1058). Steelkilt exhibited his natural superiority by remaining calm and attempting to take refuge in a countervailing convention, pointing to the three boys who were the "customary sweepers" (1058). Radney persisted, repeating his command and threatening Steelkilt with a hammer. Neither man backed down, Steelkilt warning Radney not to touch him with that hammer; when Radney did, Steelkilt broke his jaw with a punch. That would make it harder for Radney to issue orders, for a while.

Though justified by natural right, Steelkilt had no illusions about the hazards of having violated the legal conventions of the ship. He went for reinforcement to his two "comrades"—"Canallers," that is, sailors who had worked on the Erie Canal and thus would have a certain social connection with a sailor who had worked on the Great Lakes (1059). This requires Ishmael to offer another explanation to his Spanish friends, who have never ventured into North America. The Erie Canal has many of the characteristics of the Great Lakes. It may be narrow but it is very long—360 miles "through the entire breadth of the state of New York," with cities and villages, swamps and "affluent, cultivated fields," vast forests, "noble Mohawk counties" but also "rows of snow-white chapels, whose spires stand almost like milestones" (1059–1060). "Snow-white" gives the reader pause, and indeed there is a touch of the Whale's chaos even along the Canal. It consists of "one continuous stream of Venetianly corrupt and often lawless life," a point on which Ishmael does not fail to recur to his schoolmasterly inclination to offer a lesson: "There howl your pagans; where you ever find them, next door to you; under the far-flung shadow, and the snug patronizing lee of churches. For by some curious fatality, as it is often noted of your metropolitan freebooters that they ever encamp around the halls of justice, so sinners, gentlemen, most abound in holiest vicinities" (1060).

At this point, a silent and unnamed listener interrupts, confirming Ishmael's understanding of fatality. Acknowledging the guest's courtesy in referring to "distant Venice" instead of "present Lima," this self-professed native of Lima cites "the proverb all along this coast—'Corrupt as Lima.'" The citizens of Lima have self-knowledge, perhaps more than the citizens of the United States. The man is a sailor, too, saying he's seen Venice—indeed as corrupt as Ishmael has claimed: "The holy city of the blessed evangelist, St. Mark!—St. Dominic, purge it!" he exclaims. Dominic founded a new and austere order within the Catholic Church, a new regime within that regime. Does New York State need a new regime? Can a redirected "New America" give it one?

His veracity affirmed and encouraged, Ishmael continues his portrait of the Canallers, men as "abundantly picturesque and wicked" as heroes in dramas; "like Mark Antony" (another revolutionary) along the Canal, the Yankee Nile, the Canaller "indolently floats, openly toying with his red-cheeked Cleopatra" (1060); Shakespeare describes the original Cleopatra as having her cheeks alternately cooled and warmed by the fans her slaves wave over her. (It must be admitted that this wasn't the last time a sailor would hail a whore aboard ship, in the hope of having his breath taken away.) "But ashore, all this effeminacy is dashed," as he plays the "terror to the smiling innocence of the villages through which he floats." Nonetheless, as with so many rough-edged men, including Steelkilt and even Radney, the Canaller has his "redeeming qualities," proving as ready "to back a poor stranger in a strait, as to plunder a wealthy one" (1060). One such befriended Ishmael, who evidently had gotten himself into a strait at some point. Given these characteristics, Canallers are as much "distrusted by our whaling captains" as Aussies, proverbially a rough lot. "To many thousands of our rural boys and young men born along its line, the probationary life of the Grand Canal furnishes the sole transition between quietly reaping in a Christian corn-field, and recklessly ploughing the waters of the most barbaric seas" (1061).

Don Pedro understands. "No need to travel! The world's one Lima. I had thought, now, that at your temperate North the generations were cold and holy as the hills (1061). He urges digressing Ishmael to get back to the story.

In the ensuing shipboard brawl, Steelkilt and the Canallers fought two junior mates and four harpooneers, with other sailors joining in. Safely removed to the sidelines, "the valiant captain danced up and down with a whale-pike, calling upon his officers to manhandle that atrocious scoundrel," but without much effect, as "Steelkilt and his desperadoes were too much for them all" (1061). Barricading himself and his allies, Steelkilt opened negotiations, offering to return to work if the captain guaranteed no flogging: "Treat us decently," he told the captain, "and we're your men" (1062). Faced with this crisis of authority, this conflict of natural justice with the need to enforce convention, the captain refused; eventually Steelkilt and the other (now) nine mutineers agreed to be confined to the forecastle, where over the next five days the captain starved out all but the original three. At this point, Steelkilt proposed a breakout and a shipboard rampage but the Canallers betrayed him, tied him up, handed him over. For their pains, all of them were tied to the mizzen rigging, where the Canallers hung on either side of Steelkilt, like "the two crucified thieves" with Christ (1065). Ishmael thus presents his Spanish-Catholic friends with a serious parody of the Crucifixion, a version suggesting that the Apostles betrayed Christ (as indeed one of them did, albeit for money). The parody preserves the nobility of the would-be savior of the ship from the tyrannical first mate and lackluster captain. But that nobility has a serpentine quality; this 'Christ' has a certain devilry in him. As the captain prepares to flog the offender against the law of the ship, Steelkilt "hissed out something, inaudible to all but the Captain," who hesitates and then desists. At this, Radney arose from his birth; hissed at similarly by Steelkilt, he hesitated but flogged him anyway. What is the meaning of this serpentine hiss?

It may have something to do with the result of Steelkilt's failed revolution. Could he have whispered to the officers that his flogging would cause a violent revolt? However this may be, he had now won over the crew, effecting a real revolution underneath the superficial return to order. At his insistence, however, the sailors did not mutiny overtly, in action. He persuaded them rather to desert the ship after it reached port, and in the meantime to refuse to shout out if they sight a whale. In thus subverting the purpose of the regime by the means of a new social compact, Steelkilt destroyed the rule of his erstwhile masters. There shall be no "Town-ho!" cry on the *Town-Ho*, the men agreed. Thoreau-like civil disobedience will preserve the ship physically, maintain its regime nominally, while ending the regime effectively. Steelkilt has exacted public revenge on tyranny, with the prudence of a natural ruler.

Even so, as a man of still excessive spiritedness, an imperfect founder, Steelkilt wasn't done with his private enemy. He plotted to murder Radney by smashing his head with an iron ball. Here the promised "wondrous, inverted visitation of one of those so called judgments of God" occurred. "A fool saved the would-be murderer from the bloody deed he planned," but simultaneously provided him with the means of "complete revenge" (1068). Revenge is mine, saith the LORD of the Bible; "by a mysterious fatality, Heaven itself seemed to step in to take out of his hands into its own the damning thing he would have done." This begins with the action of the salvific fool, "forgetful of the compact among the crew," who saw none other than Moby-Dick, and blurted out, "There she rolls!" (1068) Social compacts can prove vulnerable to the passion of the moment. This cry united the crew, sailors, and officers alike, "anxious to capture so famous and precious a fish." Ishmael again calls attention to the "strange fatality pervad[ing] the whole career of these events, as if verily mapped out before the world itself was charted"—as if providential, as if planned as Ahab in his cabin had planned, and as God does plan, according to the Bible (1068). Fatality evidently works through the natural human desires for fame and fortune. We draw our maps, but Fate can and may redraw them.

The whale-boats dropped into the sea and pursued the Whale. Radney ordered his crew to row right up to it, and Moby-Dick killed him for his zeal. Chaotic nature has its graces, even as rough Lakemen and Canallers have their virtues. Steelkilt, who crewed on Radney's boat, cut the harpoon line, setting Moby-Dick free—one good turn deserving another. For his part, Moby-Dick eluded the other boats and disappeared; having done injury only to the petty tyrant who threatened him, the Whale injured no one else. Chaotic nature even has its justice, on occasion. Indeed, it might be argued, as this yarn-within-the yarn suggests, that Moby-Dick harms no human being who does not attempt to kill him, that the dreaded monster of the deep, and even the horrific chaos-cosmos he represents, only lashes out at its human tormentors.

Steelkilt would need one more intervention from providential chaos. Safely reaching the island, he and several others did desert, as planned. Undermanned, the beleaguered captain set out for Tahiti, some 500 miles distant, "to procure a reinforcement to his [depleted] crew" (1070). Steelkilt intercepted his boat, forced the captain to delay his mission for six days, then set out for Tahiti himself. He and his just, secessionist revolutionaries found two ships soon to sail for France, land of revolutionaries, ships whose captains were "providentially in want of precisely that number of men which the sailor headed" (1070). Ten days later, the captain arrived on his boat, recruited some Tahitians, returned to his island-haven, and "resumed his cruisings" (1071). In effect, Steelkilt (with an assist from chaos) had saved both himself from hanging and the whale ship from tyranny. The "town" or confirmed whale sighting on the *Town-Ho* aids revolution in the 'town,' the change of its regime. (As for the earliest English-language meaning of the word, 'town' as 'garden,' it will figure later in Ishmael's yarn.) Six is the number of God's initial days of work. An inversion, indeed: Steelkilt required of the captain six days of rest in order to complete his own prudential and providential revolutionary action.

No one knows where Steelkilt is now, Ishmael reports. In Nantucket, Radney's widow mourns her lost husband; like Ahab's wife, she might have been among the worshippers at the Whalemen's Chapel. Ishmael swears in front of a priest, on a copy of the Gospels, that his yarn is "in substance and its great items, true" (1072); he knew members of the *Town-Ho*'s crew, and had met and talked with Steelkilt himself. It is of course questionable how seriously Ishmael would swear upon the Gospels, that most telling yarn which he has parodied in his own. But in substance and its great items, there is no reason to doubt that his yarn weaves true to his own considered convictions.

At last the secret is out. The sailors on the *Pequod* prudently kept this yarn from the hearing of Ahab and his officers (formal and real) because it shows not only that revolution against tyranny can succeed but how it can succeed. Regime change requires courage, prudence, and assistance from both fellow-subjects and from a force stronger than any human reckoning can fathom or any human action can control. But it can be done. Steelkilt did not aspire to rule the whale ship, only to get free of its tyrannical regime, a regime that invited him to revolt in a manner similar to that described by Hegel in his passage on the struggle for "recognition" between slave and master. Success here required not isolation but alliance, and indeed loyalty in combat. The wrong or private revenge was prevented by a sort of pre-destination, whether providential or fated. Ishmael here calls it providence, but he's talking with pious Spanish Catholics. This notwithstanding, here is a sort of justice in small parts of the chaotic war of all against all that animates life both at sea and on land. If that were not so, could we trust Ishmael the yarn-spinner at all, or Melville? Could we trust ourselves to learn from them?

*Chapter Seven*
# WHALES AND WHALE-HUNTING

Having reintroduced Moby-Dick, Melville devotes the next sixteen chapters
to whales and whale-hunting. This pattern—a gam between the *Pequod*
and another whale ship, followed by a yarn about whaling, brief times of
peace followed by long periods of war—will prevail for the second half of
the book. It follows the refined understanding of the cosmos Ishmael introduced in the middle of his yarn, his suggestion that even chaos features
a few safe harbors, a few island havens.

This set of chapters concerns bodies, and it is the nature of things for
bodies to devour bodies. It begins with three chapters on the bodies of
whales as depicted in paintings and other visual media. "Such pictures of
whales are all wrong"—"pictorial delusions" whose "primal source" or
sources may be found among Hindu, Egyptian, and Greek sculpture
(1073). Those were "inventive but unscrupulous times" (as Melville has already asserted with respect to ancient sculptures) and "ever since then has
something of the same sort of license prevailed, not only in the most popular pictures of the whale, but in many scientific presentations of him"
drawn by men who were looking at beached whales mutilated and de-
formed by whatever catastrophes had killed them (1073). A beached whale
is the proverbial fish out of water, and so the whole of it as it is in life "must
remain unpainted to the last" (1077). "The only mode in which you can
derive even a tolerable idea of his living contour, is by going a whaling yourself," a hazardous expedition; "it seems to me you had best not be too fas-
tidious in your curiosity touching this Leviathan" (1077). Experience is the
best way of knowing, but, as Radney's fate shows, getting close enough for
detailed observation risks killing the observer. Among painters, the "less er-
roneous" efforts have been undertaken by the French generally, and by Am-
broise Loui Garneray in particular. "The French are the lads for painting
action," evidently because they have long been the preeminent military

power in Europe (1079). Although Ishmael professes not to know it, Garneray, though never a whaler, served as an officer in the French navy during the Napoleonic Wars. By contrast, industrial and commercial "English and American draughtsmen seem entirely content with presenting the mechanical outline of things, such as the vacant profile of the whale" (1080). Regimes enter into the souls of artists as much as they do the souls of whalemen.

Civilization itself may interfere with artists who attempt to capture the whale. The proof is in our yarn-spinner himself, portrayer of whales in words. "Long exile from Christendom and civilization inevitably restores a man to that condition in which God placed him, *i.e.* what is called savagery. Your true whale-hunter is as much a savage as an Iroquois. I myself am a savage"—an outsider, an Ishmael (1082). This matters, not necessarily (as one might suppose) because the primal, savage man best understands the primal, savage beast but because "one of the peculiar characteristics of the savage in his domestic hours, is his wonderful patience of industry" (1083). With that patience, "the white sailor-savage [...] will carve you a bit of bone sculpture, not quite as workmanlike, but as close packed in its maziness of design, as the Greek savage, Achilles' shield" and "as full of barbaric spirit and suggestiveness, as the prints of that fine old German savage, Albert Dürer" (1083). Ishmael and his maker, Melville, exhibit similar patience, similar barbarity or "so-called" savagery, similar attention to detail. Such men will show you the whale, without endangering your body although perhaps endangering your mind.

As for the whale's body, the Right Whale nourishes it with brit, tiny crustaceans that live on the surface of the ocean. "Brit" is the chapter containing the middle pages of the book, and in them we learn that "to landsmen in general, the native inhabitants of the seas have ever been regarded with emotions unspeakably unsocial and repelling"; Columbus, for example, "sailed over numberless unknown worlds to discover his one superficial western one" (1086). Such surface-sailing induces the illusion of mastery, seen especially in the modern attempt to conquer nature itself. But "however baby man may brag of his science and skill, and however much, in a flattering future, that science and skill may augment; yet for ever and for ever, to the crack of doom, the sea will insult and murder him, and pulverize the stateliest, stiffest frigate he can make" (1086). The illusion of modern science, and of the civilization that preens itself on its supposed triumph over savagery, brings men to lose "that sense of the full awfulness of the sea which aboriginally belongs to it." For we overlook what should be an obvious fact: "Noah's flood has not yet subsided; two thirds of the fair world it yet covers" (1086). And that two-thirds of the world devours not only land and landsmen who venture onto it but itself. The sea "is also fiend to its own offspring," "dash[ing] even the mightiest whales upon the rocks" along with wrecked ships. "No mercy, no power but its own controls it": Where is God, Ishmael implies, on the ocean? Has God ever moved across the waters of the primeval cosmos? "The masterless ocean overruns the globe." But more, the ocean's power finds its match in the ocean's "subtlety." "Its most dreaded creatures glide under water." Like the cosmos itself, its lovely, azure surface hides monsters, and those monsters themselves come in forms of "devilish brilliance and beauty." Hobbes had it right: a place of "universal cannibalism," the sea shelters creatures which "prey upon each other, carrying on eternal war since the world began" (1087).

And then consider yourself, know yourself as well as a native of Lima knows his city. "Do you not find a strange analogy to something in yourself" in this war of all against all, in and on the sea that surrounds the land? As "this appalling ocean surrounds the verdant land, so in the soul of man there lies one insular Tahiti"—one place where desperate captains and their mutinous crewmen both find respite—"full of peace and joy, but encompassed by all the horrors of the half known life. God keep thee! Push not off from that isle, thou canst never return!" Who is the God who might preserve you in this Eden within yourself? He does not seem to be on the waters, but He does seem to be (even if only as a metaphor) in the cautionary tale of Ishmael's yarn, words both illustrating and exemplifying the deliberation and choice that can inflect if not master or rule fate and chance. Self-knowledge and consequent self-protection are still possible, even if the conquest of nature for the relief of man's estate never really has been and never really will be. Central to *Moby-Dick* stands this challenge to the Bible and to religions generally, and to American, Western, and modern rationalism, along with a classical, 'ancient,' and reasonable reply, wrapped though it may be in 'Romantic' rhetoric.

One may measure the difference between the Right Whale and the Sperm Whale by noticing that the former eats brit, the latter giant squid.

As the *Pequod* sailed toward Java, the Spirit-Spout occasionally beckoning them on, Daggoo sighted what appeared to be Moby-Dick. It turned out to be a giant squid, basking on the surface. As with its enemy, the Sperm Whale, "few [men] have any but the most vague ideas concerning [the giant squid's] true nature and form" (1089). Sailors suppose that it clings to the bottom of the ocean with its giant tentacles, only to be pried loose and devoured by the Sperm Whale, which, unlike the Right Whale, has the jaw and the teeth necessary for that task. But it is "only by inference" that "one can tell of what, precisely," the Sperm Whale's food consists (1090). Ahab did not care. As soon as the squid was identified, he silently turned his boat back to the ship. Tyrant Ahab plots; he never wonders. Ever-observant, prudent Queequeg matter-of-factly remarked that where you see squid you will see the Sperm Whale.

Ishmael turns next to the business of killing whales. Each harpoon attaches to a "whale-line," the rope that "folds the whole boat in its complicated coils, twisting and writhing around it in almost ever direction," like the deadly snakes draped around Indian jugglers" (1093). With a harpooned whale pulling it, the line may entangle a sailor and drag him overboard. This should terrorize the men, "yet habit—strange thing! What cannot habit accomplish?"—enables them to laugh and joke, even as the boat itself "rock[s] like a cradle," pitching each one from side to side (1093). Ahab understood the power of habit as a tool of everyday ruling; here it faces down the prospect of death. But consider yourself, Ishmael again recommends: "All are born with halters around their necks; but it is only when caught in the swift, sudden turn of death, that mortals realize the silent, subtle, ever-present perils of life" (1094). A philosopher would feel no more or less terror in a whale boat than in a chair before his hearth. The hemorrhage, the embolism, the seizure: Just as every human being has his inner Tahiti, so has he his death-dealing, serpentine, inner chaos.

Queequeg was right. They sighted a whale. In the pursuit it dove, surfacing near Stubb's boat. Ishmael provides a blood-soaked description of the kill, not omitting the whipping of the line in the boat. The whale's "tormented body rolled not in brine but in blood, which bubbled and seethed for furlongs behind in their wake. The slanting sun playing upon this crimson pond in the sea, sent back its reflection into every face, so that they all glowed to each other like red men," their savage forebears in the whaling life (1098–1099). Stubb ordered the men to pull the whale to the surface, then took a lance and probed for its heart. "At least, gush after gush of clotted red gore, as if it had been the purpose lees of red wine, shot into the frighted air"; Stubb's lance had burst the whale's heart. All in a day's work for Stubb, who paused to dump the dead ashes of his pipe into the water, "thoughtfully eyeing the vast corpse he had made." It will soon transpire that he contemplated not the cosmos but the prospect of dinner.

The time between the kill and the meal gives Ishmael time to propose a modest reform in whaling practices. Harpooneers are expected not only to hit the whale but to join in rowing the whale-boat. This tires them, contributing to the poor percentage of kills—only five of fifty throws fastens the harpoon firmly on the whale. If the (as it were) spiritual side of Ishmael seeks its inner Tahiti, the practical side aims not at revolution but at reform. For him, given his assessment of nature, modest self-government prevails in thought and action.

Mr. Stubb concerned himself more with eating—brit for Right Whales, Squid for Sperm Whales, Sperm Whales for himself. While Ahab viewed the kill with "some vague dissatisfaction, or impatience, or despair," being no nearer to killing Moby-Dick, Stubb, "flushed with conquest, betrayed an unusual but still good-natured excitement." ("Staid Starbuck, his official superior, quietly resigned to him for the time the sole management of affairs"—a resignation to which that good man may too readily recur (1104–1105).) Temporarily free of rule by his two superiors, Stubb ordered Daggoo to cut him a steak from the prime section of the whale. He was not the only creature dining with relish, however, as the sharks swarmed around the carcass, gouging out their own filets. Ishmael sharply observes that sharks follow slave ships, too, devouring the bodies of dead slaves, tossed overboard. For his entertainment before dining, Stubb commanded the ship's black cook, himself effectively a slave, to deliver a sermon to the sharks, to tell them to quiet their thrashing. Unamused by the command to perform what amounted to a minstrel show for the Second Mate, Christian "Fleece" had no choice but to obey, preaching very much along the lines Ishmael himself thinks. Addressing the sharks as "fellow-critters," he admitted that their voracity "can't be helped" because "dat is natur"; perhaps thinking more of Stubb than of the heedless sharks, he added that "to govern wicked natur, dat is de pint," since angels themselves are "not'ing more dan de shark well goberned" (1108). And (again thinking of Stubb, who shared his meal with no one) could you not add a bit of charity and justice to your actions? Turning directly to Stubb, Fleece announced that it was no use, that sharks "don't hear one word," and will feed until their bellies are full—except that their "bellies is bottomless." This is one lesson Stubb does take from the designated sermonizer: "Upon my soul, I am about of the same opinion," and so will go to dinner (1109). After listening to several peremptory orders for more whale-meat tomorrow, gentle-souled, lamblike Fleece judged Stubb to be no better than a shark.

Ishmael concurs, widening the lesson, Montaigne-like, to mankind generally. Just as we are all savages, beneath the civilizational surface, so we are all cannibals. "Go to the meat-market of a Saturday night and see the crowds of live bipeds staring up at the long rows of dead quadrupeds" (1113–1114). But why does that make men cannibals, rather than merely voracious?

Ishmael shows why he thinks so as he describes the "laborious" business of what later generations of slaughterers decorously call 'processing' the whale. Queequeg and another sailor killed some of the sharks, an effort which "brought about new revelations of the incredible ferocity of the foe" (1115). Sharks began to devour the bowels of the sharks ripped open by the whale-spades; more, the disemboweled sharks ate their own bowels "till those entrails seemed swallowed over and over again by the same mouth." Here is pantheism, indeed: nature is self-devouring; it cannibalizes itself and derives energy from that very cannibalism. "A sort of generic or Pantheistic vitality seemed to lurk in their very joints and bones, after what might be called the individual life had departed" (1115). No isolatoes in nature, but no sweet pantheism of peace, either: Neither Percy Bysshe Sehlley nor Ralph Waldo Emerson ever went to sea. Ishmael gives Queequeg the coda, a serious wisecrack: "Queequeg no care what god made him shark"—readers will recall Blake's "tyger," the animal to which Fedallah's crew were compared—"wedder Feejee god or Nantucket god; but da god wat made shark must be one dam Ingin"—savage, blood-red, like the faces of the sailors when the sun reflected the bloody water (1116).

Attuned to the Laws of Nature and of Nature's God, the whalemen ignore the Sabbath, working on the whale that Sunday, "every sailor a butcher," bloodied (1117). The Sabbath separates the day of rest from the days of work, even as the Creator-God of the Bible remains separate from His Creation. But in a pantheistic cosmos no genuine separation exists; one day is like another, distinguished only by the kind of actions undertaken on that day. The upper blubber-layer of the whale is called the "blanket-piece," and indeed serves to insulate the whale in all hemispheres, and in the depths of the ocean (1118). The blubber came off the corpse like an orange rind. This unforbidden fruit was thrown into the ship's blubber-room. "Into this twilight apartment sundry nimble hands kept coiling away the long blanket-pieces as if it were a great live mass of plaited serpents" (1118). In the pantheistic cosmos, fruit and Serpent are essentially the same thing, things to be 'processed' and 're-processed.' In the pantheistic chaos, all persons, animals, and things are at least in some measure blood-red "dam Ingins."

The Sperm Whale's thick, dense blubber does act like a blanket "or, better still, an Indian poncho" (1121). "Crossed and re-crossed with numberless straight lines" resembling hieroglyphs, whale blubber features a pattern which reminds Ishmael of "those mysterious cyphers on the walls of pyramids" (in Egypt, where God's people were enslaved) and also "the old Indian characters chiseled on the famous hieroglyphic palisades on the banks of the Upper Mississippi." "Like those mystic rocks, too, the mystic-marked whale remains indecipherable" (1120). If God is indeed "a dam Ingin," His inscrutable actions (whether in making tigers, lambs, or sharks) match the inscrutability of the markings He leaves. His Word is no-word, or at least no word understandable by any person now alive. But the whale also shares with humans lungs and warm blood. The blanket protects "the great monster" from the cold of deep and far-northern waters and the tropical heat. "It does seem to me," Ishmael testifies, "that herein we see the rare virtue of a strong individual vitality, and the rare virtue of thick walls, and the rare virtue of interior spaciousness. Oh, man! Admire and model thyself after the whale! Do thou, too remain warm among ice. Do thou, too, live in this world without being of it." Ishmael clarifies this Christian thought with a classical coda: "In all seasons retain a temperature of thine own" (1121). Here is the lesson of Fleece's sermon, heard not by a shark but by a fellow-human. Once again, Ishmael commends defense of the inner Tahiti against chaos. Melville's contemporary, Nietzsche, would soon call for a pessimism of strength; Melville's Ishmael already has a (pantheistic) pessimism of strength.

He returns to his account of whaling's laborious business. The sailors separated the body of the whale from its valuable head, cutting the body loose from the ship and leaving it to drift. It was white, like "a marble sepulcher" and of course like the living death, Moby-Dick. "Beneath the unclouded and mild azure sky, upon the fair face of the pleasant sea, wafted by the joyous breezes, that great mass of death floats on and on, till lost in infinite perspectives," "flesh consumed by sea-gulls," "the air-sharks all punctiliously in black or speckled," examples of the "horrible vulturism of earth from which not the mightiest whale is free" (1123). The whale lived on, however, in the superstitious minds of sailors. Seen from afar by "some timid man-of-war or blundering discovery-vessel," the "whale's unharming corpse" is often mistaken for a shoal or a rock, the region set down in a log book as a danger zone, avoided for years by other ships, which "leap over it as silly sheep leap over a vacuum, because their leader originally leaped there when a stick was held." (1123) Sheep bring Christians to mind, and indeed, Ishmael scornfully exclaims, "There's your law of precedents; there's your utility of traditions; there's the story of your obstinate survival of old beliefs never bottomed on the earth, and now not even hovering in the air! There's orthodoxy!" (1123–1124) It is a funeral dirge not for the whale but for religion. "Thus, while in life the great whale's body may haves been a real terror to his foes, in his death his ghost becomes a powerless panic to a world"—specifically, the world of those who believe unwittingly false reports carefully written down as well-intended warnings to the flock (1124). Ghostly horror-stories, like idealistic fantasies, like the beautiful surface of the world itself, only mask reality, diverting men from attention to what they most need to know.

Ahab thought of the whale-head as a sphinx. Reversing the legend, it never interrogated him; he interrogated it, or rather entreated and even prayed to it. "Tell us the secret thing that is in thee," what you have learned, you who have "moved amid this world's foundations," the primeval water over which the God of the Bible moved. You have seen not only the foundation of the world but the human beings who have lived and died above it: the drowned sailors; the lovers who jumped from the burning ship; the murder-victims of pirates. "O head! thou hast seen enough to split the planets and make an infidel of Abraham," the most faithful of the faithful, "and not one syllable is thine!" (1126–1127) In the legend, the answer to the

Sphinx's riddle is "Man." In this more real world, the Sphinx remained silent, giving no answers. Lapsed-Quaker Ahab longed for St. Paul to come, "and to my breezelessness bring his breeze," the Holy Spirit. "O nature, and O soul of man! how far beyond all utterance are your linked analogies!"— those parallels between the atomistic material of the macrocosm and the microcosm, the mind of man (1127). In the materialist and pantheist chaos there is no creating *Logos*, no understandable Word of God. The response to man's questions, whether addressed to God or nature, is silence.

The next gam closes this account of cosmic cannibalism with an ironic answer to Ahab's prayer. The Sphinx did not speak, but it had a sort of prophet. The crew sighted the *Jeroboam*, another whale-ship out of Nantucket. Captain Mayhew refused to board the *Pequod*, as his own crew suffered from an epidemic. He preferred to converse with Ahab from a whale-boat. The original Jeroboam, the evil king of southern Israel portrayed in 1 Kings 11–14, has his counterpart not in the captain but in a crazed Shaker who accompanied him on the boat, a man with "deep, settled delirium" in his eyes, who has neutralized the legitimate rule of the captain and his officers by terrifying the crew with end-times prophecies. The madman came from the "crazy society of Niskayuna Shakers," who settled in that upstate New York village in 1774, in order to bring the sect's founder, Mother Ann Lee, recently arrived from England via New York City, to a safe haven (1129). (Judging from one extant portrait, Mother Lee, it might be noted, had an extraordinarily prominent forehead, rather resembling that of a sperm whale.) At Niskayuna, this man had "announced the speedy opening of the seventh vial" of the Book of Revelation, which was in this case "supposed to be charged with laudanum." But he soon departed for Nantucket, seized with still another "strange, apostolic whim." "With that cunning peculiar to craziness, he assumed a steady, common sense exterior," enabling him to sign on to the whaling ship; safely out of sight of land, he "announced himself as the archangel Gabriel [meaning "God is my strength"], guardian angel of Israel and trumpeter of the world's doom, "commanding the captain to jump overboard" (1129–1130). Although the captain disobeyed, he found himself increasingly powerless, as "the dark, daring play of his sleepless, excited imagination, and all the preternatural terrors of real delirium, united to invest this Gabriel in the minds of the majority of the ignorant crew, with an atmosphere of sacredness" and feelings of terror. "Jeroboam" means "the people contend," and so they did, effectively mutinying, changing the regime of the ship from a monarchy to a popularly-supported tyranny. (The name "Mayhew" might be a sly reference to Jonathan Mayhew, an eminently respectable New England clergyman of the Founding Era who blended liberal Christianity with sober Lockeanism, the sort of man who may indeed influence the course of events on stable, dry land but find himself all at sea, when at sea with a self-proclaimed prophet of God.) The epidemic only increased 'Gabriel's' usurped authority, as he "declar[ed] that the plague, as he so called it" (following Biblical language) "was at his sole command; nor should it be stayed but according to his good pleasure" (1130). After proclaiming Moby-Dick to be God, 'Gabriel' correctly prophesied the death of the First Mate, who had announced his intention to kill the Whale; this confirmed his authority over the "poor devils," the crew. From then on, the crew "sometimes render[ed] him personal homage, as to a god," of whom they begged for mercy. In the Bible, Jeroboam leads Israel in idolatrous worship of the Golden Calf. The new Jeroboam is his own prophet, priest, king, and Golden Calf, all in one.

Much of this parallels much of Ahab's own tyranny. From his feigned sanity to gain access to the ship, to his usurpation of the authority of the owners of the *Pequod* once safely offshore, to his dominance over the officers by mesmeric words of monomaniacal ardor that bring the crew under his tyrannical rule, 'Gabriel' does indeed answer Ahab's prayer by holding a mirror up to him. After hearing Ahab also intended to kill the Whale, he prophesied Ahab's destruction: "Beware the blasphemer's end!" (1132) "The crazy sea […] seemed in league with him" (1131)—a just analogy, indeed, as 'Gabriel' will prove a true prophet not of God but of chaos, even as he has ruled superstitious men by means of an idolatrous, self-divinizing cult. The Biblical Jeroboam waged constant war with the house of Judah, the king of northern Israel. Both Israels finally deviated from the God of the Bible, as indeed the "houses" of the *Pequod* and the *Jeroboam* have done. "Curses throttle thee!" Ahab shrieked in reply (1133). The war of the two false Israels continued.

## Chapter Eight
# ISOLATOES NO MORE

Ishmael has shown how a man might prudently choose to mark out and preserve his inner core within the pantheist chaos. This would make him a more tranquil isolato, but still an isolato—one of Tocqueville's "individualists," living precariously because alone. In the next ten chapters, he shows how such men might cooperate with like men. The sequence leads up to the *Pequod's* first encounter that tests whether this tentative sociality might extend to other nations, other regimes.

Ishmael had already established a friendship with Queequeg, and readers have seen the soundness of his choice. During the operation of stripping blubber from the whale, Queequeg stood on the corpse's slippery back, attached to Ishmael, who remained on deck, by the "monkey-rope," tied to the belt of each man (1134). As the stripping proceeded, waves jostled the corpse against the side of the ship; Ishmael's task was to steady his friend, to prevent him from falling and being crushed. He had every reason to take care, quite apart from the bond of friendship, for if Queequeg slid off he would pull Ishmael overboard. Unique to the *Pequod*, the notion of the monkey-rope arose in the fertile mind of Stubb, who calculated that such a device would ensure vigilance in the man on deck by appealing to the low but solid ground of self-preservation.

Although far from incognizant of this point, Ishmael also recalled their 'marriage' (now indeed 'for better or for worse') and further compared their pairing to Siamese twin-ship. More, "So strongly and metaphysically did I conceive of my situation then, that while earnestly watching his motions, I seemed distinctly to perceive that my own individuality was now merged in a joint stock company of two: that my free will had received a mortal wound; and that another's mistake or misfortune might plunge innocent me into unmerited disaster and death" (1135). Unjust as this interdependence might be, it precluded any thoughts of isolation, whether terrifying or tranquil.

And as a matter of fact, he saw, "this situation of mine was the precise situation of every mortal that breathes": "If your banker breaks, you snap; if your apothecary by mistake sends you poison in your pills, you die" (1135). There are no real isolatoes. Self-government of the human soul can be established, but self-government in action requires alert cooperation. "Handle Queequeg's monkey-rope heedfully as I could, sometimes he jerked it so, that I came very near sliding overboard. Nor could I possibly forget that, to do what I would, I only had the management of one end of it" (1135).

Chaos remained the enemy of all this, as the sharks continued to swarm around the corpse "like bees round […] a beehive" (1136). Fellow-harpooneers Tashtego and Daggoo attempted to kill as many of them as possible with their whale-spades, and while "they meant Queequeg's best happiness," the "indiscreet spades" they wielded "would come nearer to amputating a leg than a tail" (1136). Is Queequeg "not the precious image of each and all of us men in this whaling world? That unsounded ocean you gasp in, is Life; those sharks, your foes; those spades, your friends; and what between sharks and spades you are in a sad pickle, and peril, poor lad" (1136). Sentiment alone cannot meet the dangers of chaos; the best of friends need to bring observation, prudence, and skill with it. Ishmael ends his reflection on friendship with a glance at the other extreme of ineffectual sentiment. When cold and exhausted Queequeg returned safely to the deck, and the hapless deck-hand, Dough-boy, offered him a ginger drink, provided to the crew by teetotaling Aunt Charity, back in Nantucket. This earned a sharp reproof from Stubb, who sensibly ordered grog for the man, instead. Charity, yes; foolish, Christian-temperance charity, no.

With the Sperm Whale's head still attached to one side of the ship, Ahab ordered the crew to chase and kill a Right Whale and to tie it to the *Pequod*'s other side, for balance. Flask told Stubb that he overheard Fedallah recommending this, a report that moved the Second Mate to call the Parsee "the devil in disguise." Ahab has made a deal with the devil, Stubb feared, and he blames God for allowing the devil to prowl the earth, "kidnapping people" (1141). However this may be, the Ahab-Fedallah twin-ship forms a shadow-parallel with the friendship of Ishmael and Queequeg. And in a way literally so: Fedallah stood at the edge of the deck, looking at the Right Whale's head and evidently finding an analogy between its wrinkles and the lines of his hand—that is, his fate. By chance, Ahab stood nearby at such an angle that "the Parsee occupied his shadow," blending with it and making it longer (1144). The superstitious crew continued its work, but "Laplandish speculations were bandied among them"; pantheists and animists, ruled by a shaman, the ancient Laplanders parallel the modern whale-ship crew, cutting up a whale in the middle of the ocean. Ishmael considers the two whale-heads in a different, more reasonable light. "By the counterpoise of both heads," the *Pequod* "regained her even keel, though sorely strained"; "so, when on one side you hoist Locke's head"—emblem of empiricism—"you go over that way; but now, on the other side, hoist in Kant's"—emblem of idealism—"you come back again; but in a very poor plight." "Some minds for ever keep trimming boat," but the better way is to "throw all these thunderheads overboard, and then you will float light and right" (1143). When it comes to guiding your way of life, contradictory philosophic doctrines, even if balanced, cannot substitute for prudential judgment gained by experience.

Denigration of philosophic doctrine does not preclude philosophizing. Ishmael embarks on a brief voyage into what philosophers call the 'other minds' problem, a problem that he has already addressed in his observations of the many different human regimes or ways of life. Themselves effectively linked by the ship, the pair of whale-heads merit consideration along with the paired Ishmael and Queequeg, Ahab and Fedallah. Both whale species have eyes on the sides of their heads, which gives them two 'fronts' and two 'backs,' reminiscent of Rome's Janus, god of doorways. This requires a whale's brain to be "much more comprehensive, combining, and subtle than man's," one whereby "he can at the same moment of time attentively examine two distinct prospects, one on the one side of him, and the other in an exactly opposite direction (1147). These intellectual virtues notwithstanding, wall-eyed whales find themselves in a dilemma when attacked by whale-boats coming at them from several directions at once, circumstances in which their perceptions cause them "queer frights" and "helpless perplexity of volition, in which their divided and diametrically opposite powers of vision must involve them" (1147). Human pairs must operate somewhat similarly. Two heads *are* better than one, in ordinary circumstances, providing that they are coordinate. But two heads may prove a handicap in emergencies, when the need to act fast leaves no time for coordination, unless practice has perfected coordination in advance.

If the eye is a portal of thoughts, the ear is a portal of beliefs, of things 'seen' in the 'mind's eye,' second-hand. The ears of both species of whale are tiny; whales think, but do they believe? Sometimes worshiped by the likes of the crazed Shaker, they do not themselves worship. But, Ishmael remarks, the size of eyes and ears does not necessarily make vision or hearing more or less acute. He offers both a philosophic and a sermon-like lesson to members of his own species: "Why then do you try to 'enlarge' your mind? Subtilize it?" (1147) Then as now, educators lauded breadth of vision, all-inclusive panorama-ism of thought and of sentiment. For all his wide-ranging adventures, Melville's Ishmael prefers careful and precise thought to eclecticism, intellectual or moral.

And so he supplements these comparisons with contrasts. If "the noble Sperm Whale's head may be compared to a Roman war-chariot"—the face of Janus that looks back to the virtues of Roman aristocracy—"the Right Whale's head bears a rather inelegant resemblance to a gigantic galliot-toed shoe," likened by "an old Dutch voyager" to "a shoemaker's last"—product and tool, respectively, of the modern commercial republic (1149). This makes the Kant-and-Locke joke more precise; the more telling contrast remains that between aristocratic nobility and democratic *embourgeoisement*. Indeed, despite similarities shared by all members of the genus, "the Sperm Whale and the Right Whale have almost entirely different heads": "In the Right Whale's there is no great well of sperm"—it lacks manly fertility; "no ivory teeth at all"—nothing rare and valuable; "no long, slender mandible of a lower jaw"—betokening a warrior-spirit—but rather a mouth fitted for skimming and straining the tiny brit, the steadily but unheroically-gained profits of commercial life, a life lived mostly on the surface of things (1151). By contrast, the Sperm Whale's head hints of philosophy, its broad brow "full of a prairie-like placidity, born of a speculative indifference as to death," the "whole head seem[ing] to speak of an enormous practical resolution in facing death" (1151). Even granted the utmost nobility, the "very sulky-looking fellow," the Right Whale, "I take to have been a Stoic." But the Sperm Whale more resembles a "Platonian," a man of more elevated thinking, although he "might have taken up Spinoza in his latter years," in what one guesses to have been a move toward materialist pantheism (1152).

But what does the Sperm Whale's head do, when the whale moves from thought to action? In addition to devouring giant squid, it rams ships. "A dead, blind wall," an "enormous boneless mass" of extraordinarily tough blubber, the front of its head makes a fearsome battering-ram (1153). "Unerringly impelling this dead, impregnable, uninjurable wall [...] there swims behind it all a mass of tremendous life," "all obedient to one volition" (1154). This being so, Ishmael tells his listeners, renounce "all ignorant *in-credulity*" regarding the Sperm whale (emphasis added). Even as he attacks what he takes to be ignorant credulity, religion, Ishmael equally attacks the naïve refusal to accept reality as it is. "For unless you own the whale, you are but a provincial and sentimentalist in Truth." "What," he asked in his rhetorical clincher, "befell the weakling youth lifting the dread goddess's veil at Sais?" (1158) The goddess in question, Isis, symbolizes nature; she is veiled because nature has secrets. "I am all that has been and is and shall be," the inscription at the base of her statue tells its readers, echoing the meaning of a name of God. "No mortal has ever lifted my veil," she warns—any more than any can see God, unveiled, and live. Ishmael has met the youth in question by reading a poem by Friedrich Schiller, telling the yarn of a young quester after knowledge who does lift Isis' veil one Egyptian night, only to be found "extended, senseless, pale as death" the following morning. "Truth attained will never reward the one who unveils it," Schiller concludes. Isis is another manifestation of the Sphinx; both represent not God but chaos-nature, terrifying as the Biblical God but, in Ishmael's estimation, impersonal, a combination of fatality and chance, with a weak, faltering humanity making its often-foolish choices, easily killed in consequence of them. As for the young man, Ishmael, who has not heeded the poet's warning, or has read it too late to have heeded it, he must learn how to recover from the experience of learning the truth, having lifted the provincial and sentimental veils or conventions of his own regime. A poet's cautionary yarn can't help him, one must instead look to philosophy. But can the "Young America" bear the truth of his witness, a witness delivered in the half-poetic, monitory, half-philosophic, truth-telling, form of a novel?

Allusion to a German poet serves as a prelude. His move away from social isolation, coupled with the move toward philosophy, suggests a move toward 'Germany'—by the mid-nineteenth century home to the most celebrated philosophic critics of empiricist, 'English' materialism and individualism. The four chapters leading up to the next gam feature increasingly prominent references to German things and themes. The first such reference, "The Great Heidelberg Tun," refers to a giant wine cask that Ishmael compares to the upper part of the interior of the Sperm Whale's head. This contains substances more valuable than most German wines: The lower part, the "junk," consists of "one immense honeycomb of oil"; the upper part, the "case," contains the spermaceti—"absolutely pure, limpid, odiferous," and, it might be added, white (1156). This "tun" must be tapped carefully, "lest a careless, untimely stroke should invade the sanctuary and wastingly let out its invaluable contents" (1157). Still again, Queequeg intervened heroically in the work of the ship, rescuing Tashtego, assigned to tap the cask, who slipped and fell into the huge cavity after nearly completing his task. Ishmael describes this as an act of "obstetrics," a lesson in "midwifery" (1157). Midwifery recalls the work of Socrates, whose philosophic way of life consisted not in elaborating a doctrine or 'system' (as in the manner German philosophers tended to do) but to test or scrutinize the opinions of his fellow-citizens by engaging them in dialectical questioning, an exercise in *logos* or thought governed by the principle of non-contradiction. Socratic dialogues often not in the unveiling of truth but in *aporia,* in impasse. Queequeg's salvific action may thus be seen as a picture of Socratism.

It wasn't necessarily an endorsement of Platonism, however. Had the cask still been loaded with the spermaceti, Tashtego would have drowned, "coffined, hearsed and tombed in the secret inner chamber of the whale." "How many, think ye, have likewise fallen into Plato's honeyed head, and sweetly perished there?" (1162)

Here is another sanctuary or "inner Tahiti," even in Leviathan itself—in this 'case' both sweet and fatal, not protective. Rejecting 'Jerusalem' even as he endorses the Biblical account of the terrifying, overwhelming cosmos described in the Book of Job, Ishmael also rejects 'Athens' insofar as it features philosophers like Plato who offer (or seem to offer) a philosophic *doctrine.* Midwife Socrates may well be another matter, however. The philosopher who converses with all manner of men and boys in the agora, long-lived and courageous, an Ishmael-like outsider even as he stays physically inside the walls of his city, Socrates cannot be described as doctrinaire. Whether German philosophers lived up to Socrates' example may be doubted, as Ishmael's reference to Kant suggests. They are not superficial, to be sure, but their elaborate idea-systems may indeed be self-constructed tuns, drowning and inebriating makers and partakers alike. Socrates describes the city as a cave from which reasoned speeches may help him ascend to the light of truth; the German philosophic tuns then begin to look like tuns, or perhaps caves beneath the cave—deep but easy to get lost in, irremediably. Like the sailors on the *Pequod*, German philosophers may have embarked on a journey of no return.

The following pair of chapters satirize systematizing science, specifically the "semi-sciences" of physiognomy and phrenology. In "The Prairie" (a title recalling the "prairie-like placidity" of the Sperm Whale's brow, bespeaking indifference to death), Melville delves into physiognomy. Sperm Whales don't have noses, no facial protruberances easily pulled by demeaning jesters. Far from it: "Human or animal, the mystical brow is as that great golden seal affixed by the German emperors to their decrees," with the legend "God: done this day by my hand" (1164). The Sperm Whale's "sublime" brow gives the animal a "high and mighty god-like dignity"; viewing it, "you feel the Deity and the dread powers more forcibly than in beholding any other object in living nature," or, as a physiognomist would say, "the mark of genius" (1164). Continuing the joke, Ishmael intones, if you doubt the genius of the Sperm Whale, given his failure ever to write a book or to deliver a speech, why, "his great genius is declared in his doing nothing particular to prove it," in his "pyramidical silence" (1164). He concludes, more prosaically, "Physiology, like every other human science, is but a human fable" (1165). Again, rather like Socrates, Ishmael doubts the science of his day.

Going behind the whale's face, and on to the semi-science of phrenology, Ishmael locates its surpisingly small brain inside the monster's skull; indeed, "the most exalted potency" may prove brain-weak (1167). But consider further: "If you attentively regard almost any quadruped's spine, you will be struck with the resemblance of its vertebrae to a strung necklace of dwarf skulls, all bearing rudimentary resemblance to the skull proper" (1167). Now, "it is a German conceit, that the vertebrae are absolutely undeveloped skulls," and indeed a cannibal friend (presumably Queequeg) had observed much the same thing in the skeleton of a slain enemy. What is more, "I believe that much of a man's character will be found betokened in the backbone," as in the expression, 'He has backbone' (1167). And as a matter of fact, the whale's backbone is big and wide—not to mention its hump, an "organ of firmness and indomitableness." And indeed "the great monster is indomitable," as "you will have reason to know" (1168) Q. E. D., my listeners! The Germans would be proud.

All this Germanism leads to a gam with the *Jungfrau*, a whale-ship out of Bremen. She was a virgin, indeed, having caught no whales and having had no sightings of Moby-Dick. Captain Derick de Deer pulled his whale-boat alongside the *Pequod* with a request for some fish oil; he and his crew had yet to capture a fish of any kind at all. Celebrated as philosophic doctrinaires, the Germans are newcomers to the vast sea of experience, novices at self-government in chaos. As chance would have it, a whale pod was sighted, followed distantly by an old and feeble bull whale, slowed not only by age but by many injuries. The crews of the two ships competed in the pursuit of this shadow of the great Leviathan described in the Book of Job, which "laugheth at the shaking of a spear." But "Oh! that unfillments should follow the prophets": Leviathan can indeed by killed by men (1175).

Predictably, the *Pequod*'s crew gets to him first, there is no pity for this pitiable beast, who turns out to be blind, as well. "For all his old age, and his one arm"—he had lost a fin in some underwater fight, long ago—"he must die the death and be murdered, in order to light the gay bridals and other merry-makings of men, and also to illuminate the solemn churches that preach unconditional inoffensiveness to all" (1176). The old whale did get revenge of sorts; the crew tied it to the side of the ship, only to be forced to cut it loose (as usual, Queequeg takes this sensible, decisive action); its sheer weight threatened to drag the ship underwater. As for the *Virgin*, her captain and crew were last seen lowering the boats to chase a Fin-back Whale, a species too speedy to catch. Germans lack the judgment that comes from experience but "Oh! many are the Fin-backs, and many are the Dericks, my friend" (1179). If the Germans have rightly questioned the individualism and materialism of the English, and of the Enlightenment generally, they may have hurried off in the wrong direction, on an illusory quest of their own. This gam, this dialogue, has conducted them into an *aporia* without the dialectical advantage of having discarded illogical half-truths. They will never catch a fish that way, and they will continue to beg others for the oil that produces light.

## Chapter Nine
# PIETY AND PIRACY

The next ten chapters culminate in a gam with the second foreign whaling ship, this one from France—a major political and military power in Europe, but not so much on the seas, and not in whaling. The French had always been landsmen, unlike the Spanish, the English, and the Americans.

Ishmael's jibe at the falsehood of prophecy, following his more extensive debunking of science (the pride of modern Germany) in the previous chapter, proves a prelude to a more extensive satire on religion, rather along the line of Voltaire, that quintessential French Enlightener. He begins with a chapter on "The Honor and Glory of Whaling" (glancing slyly at the last words of the Lord's Prayer?), in which he playfully cites "the gallant Perseus, a son of Jupiter," as "the first whaleman" (1180). He then proposes that the Christian hero, St. George, slayed not a dragon but a whale. More jovially still, he announces that "by the best contradictory authorities" we learn that the story of Hercules and the whale is said to derive from "the still more ancient story of Jonah and the whale; and vice versa" (1182). Ranging farther afield, he recalls that the Hindu god Vishnu manifested himself as a whale in the first of "his ten earthly incarnations," in order to rescue the Vedas, then lying in the depths of the cosmic waters—books "whose perusal would seem to have been indispensable to Vishnoo before beginning the creation" (1182). Greek polytheism, Christianity, Judaism, and Hinduism all amount to the same thing: Each is a vehicle for a mock-exaltation of whaling and a simultaneous undermining of religious authority.

Returning to Jonah, Ishmael remarks that a Sag-Harbor whaleman doubted the story, but in so doing only "evinced the foolish pride of reason," a "foolish, impious pride, and abominable, devilish rebellion against the reverend clergy." But "old Sag-Harbor" "had but little learning except what he had picked up from the sun and the sea"—that is, experience and commonsense thinking about nature (1184). After all, not only Catholic priests but "the highly enlightened Turks devoutly believe in the historical story of Jonah" (1185). What greater testimony do we need?

Exercising knowledge picked up from the sun and the sea, Queequeg prepared his whale-boat for a chase, which occurred the next morning; such knowledge produces more reliable predictions than alleged prophecy. This incident also provides Ishmael the chance to describe another practical way to kill whales. If a whale 'runs' too far and fast to make harpooning it prudent, an experienced whaler can pitchpole it instead. He takes a long lance designed for the purpose and hurls it at the whale; instead of embedding itself deeply into the whale, the lance wounds the whale, drawing blood. The whaler pulls it back and darts the whale repeatedly, causing the whale to die the proverbial death of a thousand cuts. Insofar as Ishmael has playfully compared the Sperm-Whale to a god, it might be said that his narrative aims at causing the idea of gods as handed down by prophetic tradition and orthodox churchmen to die such a death.

Nor is Ishmael done, turning next to the pretensions of philosophers. He addresses the question of whether the whale-spout is water or mist. The whale breathes through its spiracle, not its mouth; it has a network of blood vessels which acts as a storage place for the air it takes in, when on the surface of the ocean. This allows the whale to stay submerged for long periods of time, and to dive deep. "My hypothesis is this: that the spout is nothing but mist" (1190). He bases his claim on no further empirical data, but upon "considerations touching the great inherent dignity and sublimity of the Sperm Whale," a being "both ponderous and profound," like Plato, Pyrrho, the Devil (presumably Milton's version), Dante, "and so on"—one must pause to admire that "and so on"—and therefore of the sort who emits "a certain semi-visible steam, while in the act of thinking deep thoughts" (1193). After drinking six cups of hot tea in "my thin shingled attic, of an August noon," I myself, Ishmael, find moisture in my hair, if I have been "plunged in deep thought." Not only that, but the whale-spout is often "glorified by a rainbow, as if Heaven itself had puts its seal on [the whale's] thoughts," and rainbows never "visit the clear air; they only irradiate vapor"—an observation gleaned from exact perception of experience, not from Scripture or scientific theory. In response to his own musings, Ishmael "thank[s] God": "For all have doubts; many deny; but doubts or denials, few along with them, have intuitions. Doubts of all things earthly, and intuitions of some things heavenly; this combination makes neither believer nor infidel, but makes a man who regards them both with equal eye" (1193). If science, religion, and philosophy all are dubious, then a cautious, overall agnosticism recommends itself to Melville's yarn-spinner.

Ishmael then turns to an object of unquestionable power, the Sperm Whale's tail. If whaling shares in the honor and glory owed God in the Lord's Prayer, the unspoken third word of that prayer, power, belongs to the whale, the object of the whalers' hunt. "In the tail the confluent measureless force of the whole whale seems concentrated to a point." "[T]he whole bulk of the leviathan is knit over with a warp and woof"—recall the mat Ishmael and Queequeg wove, symbol of the structure of the cosmos— "of muscular fibres and filaments," all running toward the two flukes of the tail, "contribut[ing] to their might" (1194). "Could annihilation occur to matter, this were the thing to do it," as the tail exhibits "a titanism of power," the power of the pre-Olympic gods, the pre-god gods. At the same time, even if the whale and its tail lack *l'esprit de géométrie* (generated by the brain), they do not lack *l'esprit de finesse*, as the tail undulates with ease: "Real strength never impairs beauty or harmony, but it often bestows it" (1195). Indeed, "when Angelo paints even God the Father in human form, mark what robustness is there," very much in contrast with "the soft, curled, hermaphroditical Italian pictures" of God's Son, embodying "the mere negative, feminine [power] of submission and endurance, which on all hands it is conceded, for the peculiar practical virtues of his teachings." (Machiavelli concurs, commending *lo Stato* as the more effective preserver of human lives, if not necessarily their souls.)

More, when he has seen "the gigantic tail" rising from the ocean, Ishmael thinks of "majestic Satan thrusting forth his tormented colossal claw from the flame Baltic Sea of Hell"; if in a "Dantean" mood while viewing this eruption, Ishmael envisions devils, "if in [the mood] of Isaiah, the archangels" (1197). A pod of whales heading toward the sun, with their tails momentarily uplifted in preparation for a dive, recall visions of Persian fire worshippers and, like the actions of gods, whale gestures often "remain wholly inexplicable." "Dissect him how I may, then, I but go skin deep; I know him not, and never will" (1198). And if I cannot know the tail of the whale, how shall I comprehend his front, his face, especially "when face he has none"? Like the God of the Bible, "Thou shalt see my back parts, my tail, he seems to say, but my face shall not be seen" (1198). Having satirically disposed of the grander claims of science, religion, and philosophy—of systems—Ishmael here sketches a playfully proposed but seriously intended version of 'natural religion.' Generally, this and the four previous chapters show him treating the heavy, ponderous monster, whale or god, with a light touch, with a sort of *gaya scienza* that fits the *Pequod*'s movement toward an encounter with a ship from France.

Before that encounter, the ship needed to pass through the Strait of Malacca, "the most southerly part of all Asia," and the gateway to islands holding "inexhaustible wealth of spices, and silks, and jewels, and gold, and ivory" (1199). Although the strait is easily navigable, real hazards abide there: pirates from Sumatra and Java. Although Ahab had no interest in the riches of the East, intending only to get to the prime whaling-grounds on the far coast of Japan, the pirates would attack any kind of ship. And Ahab might have needed to linger there, out of token respect for his ostensible mission; the seas off Java do promise good whale-hunting.

Ishmael titles this chapter "The Grand Armada," alluding to the Spanish expedition against England, and this seems apt. Like France (and England) Spain pioneered in building the modern, centralized state. The "armada" here consists of a confederation of whale pods. Under persistent attack by whale-ships, Sperm Whales, like feudal dynasties, often mass together; "it would almost seem as if numerous nations of them had sworn solemn league and covenant for mutual assistance and protection" (1201). The *Pequod*'s captain and crew found themselves in a double chase. To their rear, Malayan pirates pursued them; for their part, the American vessel chases an armada of whales. Ahab registered the irony. Whale-men, after all, amount to piratical raiders on the centrally-organized community— the 'modern state' or perhaps the 'empire'—of whales.

In numbers there is strength, but there is also disorder, inasmuch as the larger the community the more elements there are to coordinate. As the *Pequod* gained distance from the pirates and moved nearer the armada, the whales showed signs of panic; they were "gallied," a word derived from the same root of "gallows," and exhibiting some of the same terror gallows inspire (1204). In one of his footnotes to the novel, Melville offers an etymology of the word, arguing that it dates back to Saxon times, "emigrat[ing] to the New-England rocks with the noble brawn of the old English emigrants in the time of the Commonwealth," in a process by which "the best and furthest-descended English words"—the aristocrats of the language—"are now democratized, nay, plebeianized [...] in the New World." Gallying does in fact reflect the regime of democracy, instancing the "occasional timidity [...] characteristic of all herding creatures," not "outdone by the madness of men" (1204n.). If the whale-armada resembles a modern state or empire, its regime resembles democracy.

Queequeg harpooned a whale, which headed for the center of the armada, dragging the boat along. The crewmen needed to maneuver through the thrashing mob of panicky whales. The whale worked its way off the harpoon, and the boat glided into the center of the whale-'state.' This gave Ishmael a rare look at the inner workings of the whale's 'regime,' its way of life. "They say" an "enchanted calm lurks at the heart of every commotion," and respecting the whale armada hearsay was correct. It was "as if the cows and calves had been purposely locked up in this innermost fold," and they had found security there, "evinc[ing] a wondrous fearlessness and confidence" toward the whalers; "like household dogs they came snuffing round us, right up to our gunwales, and touching them," while allowing the sailors to touch them (1207). Mating and nursing, the whales at the center of the armada form a 'political' inner Tahiti. Ishmael recalls "the sagacious saying in the Fishery—the more whales the less fish"—and it proved so, here; the *Pequod's* boats killed only one whale on this expedition (1211). When pods band together in a large 'modern state' or 'empire,' it works as intended, providing effective defense against piratical raiders.

This 'state' does another thing modern states do: It sends out pioneers, called schools, some predominantly female, some consisting of young bulls. Typically, the female schools have "a male of full grown magnitude" as their escort or "schoolmaster," whom Ishmael compares to a harem master of the Ottoman Empire, occasionally challenged by young bulls plotting a coup; "deadly battle, all for love," ensues (1212–1213). If not deposed, the schoolmaster ages, none too gracefully. Gradually, the old ruler becomes "sulky," eventually leaving the school and becoming an isolato, who "will have no one near him but Nature herself" ("and the best of wives she is, though she keeps so many moody secrets"(1214)). His final fate has already been described: the crippling, the blindness, the feebleness of senility.

As for the schools consisting of young males, they do indeed resemble their human counterparts, "a mob of young collegians [...] full of fight, fun, and wickedness, tumbling round the world at such a reckless, rollicking rate, that no prudent underwriter would insure them any more than he would a riotous lad at Yale or Harvard" (1214–1215). These schools dissolve when the collegians become old enough to go off in search of harems. Comparing the two types of whale-school, Ishmael finds that the males will ignore a stricken fellow, but if you "strike a member of the harem school [...] her companions swim around her with every token of concern, sometimes lingering so near her and so long, as themselves to fall a prey" (1215). As with humans, the female is a more social animal than the male. Sociality without protection produces no isolatoes, but it can produce extra corpses.

Ishmael offers two more observations on piracy. The first concerns legal piracy. What happens if a whale killed by one ship get loose in a storm, floats away, and another ship salvages it? American whalers have set down a pair of simple rules: A "Fast-Fish" (one tied to a ship) belongs to the party possessing it; a "Loose-Fish" belongs to "anybody who can soonest catch it." As with all simple legal codes (as, for example, the Golden Rule, also consisting of two parts), brevity "necessitates a vast volume of commentaries to expound it," to account for special cases, the vast variety of circumstances (1216). In all this "will, on reflection, be found the fundamentals of all human jurisprudence," namely, that possession is "half of the law" and often "the whole of the law" (1218). The mansion of the criminal, the financier's usurious gains, the income of the clergyman of a poor congregation, the holdings of landed aristocrats, Ireland in relation to England ("that redoubted harpooneer"): "What are all of these if not Fast-Fish? And what was America in 1492, Poland to the Czar, Greece to the Turk, India to England, Mexico to the United States, if not Loose-Fish? More, "What are the Rights of Man and the Liberties of the World but Loose-Fish?"—up for grabs among political and military pirates. Or "all men's minds and opinions," including "the principle of religious belief in them" and "the thoughts of thinkers"—what are they to rhetoricians and sophists but Loose-Fish? Or the world? "And what are you, reader, but a Loose-Fish and a Fast-Fish, too?"—at times up for the taking, at other times a slave (1219). English royals who by law claim title to the most valuable parts of every whale and even every sturgeon captured by English ships exemplify a sovereign piracy, but piracy itself is universal.

For his final observation on piracy, Ishmael introduces a French ship which had acquired a dead whale harpooned and then lost by the *Pequod*'s crew, under the Loose-Fish doctrine. France, a home of the Enlightenment critique of religion, of modern statism, of the Rights of Man, of monarchy (at this time, and for twenty years more), and finally of Romance (*Rose-Bud* "was the romantic name of this aromatic ship," stinking of rotting whale-flesh), remains a land-power, inexperienced in whaling (1225). The French are also inexperienced when it comes to Yankee bargaining. Mr. Stubb suspects that there may be ambergris in that whale-head; he talks the French captain into cutting it loose—something the French crew does quite happily, given its smell. The French go on their way, and Stubb harvests the ambergris, prize of his "unrighteous cunning" or verbal piracy. While "this most fragrant ambergris" accumulates in "the heart of such decay," Ishmael finds no wonder in that, given the "saying of St. Paul in Corinthians, about corruption and incorruption; how that we are sown in dishonor, but raised in glory" (1230–1231). Having reduced the principle of grace to a principle of nature, Ishmael makes his own redemptive observation: "The truth is, that living or dead, if but decently treated, whales as a species are by no means creatures of ill-odor" (1232). Nor are whale-men. But to see more of that, piracy would need to decline, and under at least most possible regimes, and to some degree in all of them, the modern state tends only to replace one kind of piracy with another.

## Chapter Ten
# THE BUSINESS CYCLE

Melville now shifts his readers' attention from France to the country that defeated France. Triumphant in the Napoleonic Wars, the Great Britain of Melville's day ruled the oceans with her fleet, supporting her commerce and industry and securing her empire. In the chapters leading up to the gam with a British whaling ship out of London, Ishmael describes the effect of industrialism aboard the *Pequod.*

He begins with a yarn about Pip, "the most insignificant of the *Pequod's* crew" a diminutive free black who served, along with his white counterpart, "Dough-Boy," as a ship-keeper—one of those who stay behind on the ship when the whale boats go out on the hunt. A "most significant event" involving this most insignificant person prophesied "whatever shattered sequel" the *Pequod* itself "might" meet (1233).

Cheerful, tambourine-playing, life-loving Pip shone with exuberance on board, as he had done on the village green in his Connecticut hometown. But if a diamond exhibits a "healthful glow" in daylight, on a lady's finger, when it's still in the jeweler's shop, set against a dark background and lit by "unnatural gases," it becomes "infernally superb," "like some crown jewel stolen from the King of Hell" (1234). And so it is with bright Pip. Pressed into service on a whale boat when one of Stubb's crew was injured while collecting ambergris, he caused the Second Mate to lose a whale, partly by accident and partly out of his own panic during the chase. Stubb issued a warning: "We can't afford to lose whales by the likes of you; a whale would sell for thirty times what you would, Pip, in Alabama" (1235). The sinister light of diamonds under conditions of sale; the dangers of sharp-spading for valuable ambergris; and trafficking in human beings: Commerce promises great enhancements of vitality but exacts a price for it. As Ishmael drily remarks, "Perhaps Stubb indirectly hinted, that though man loves his fellow, yet man is a money-loving animal, which propensity too often interferes with his benevolence" (1235).

Pip soon tested the tight limits of Stubb's benevolence and patience, panicking again on the next try at a whale. He jumped overboard in fright, and Stubb, true to his brusque word, left him behind in the ocean, expecting that another boat would retrieve him. "Out from the centre of the sea, poor Pip turned his crisp, curling, black head to the sun, another lonely castaway, though the loftiest and the brightest." If Melville intends the traditional pun on sun and Son here, he suggests that the Son was forsaken, crucified, elevated to the heavens, and yet offers no salvation to man, leaving helpless Pip in the "intolerable" and "awful loneliness" of the vast Pacific Ocean (1136).

"By the merest chance the ship itself at last rescued him; but from that hour the little negro went about the deck an idiot; such, at least, they said he was. The sea had jeeringly kept his fine body up, but drowned the infinite of his soul"—almost. As in the Bible, so in Melville's novel the sea is home to "the unwarped primal world"; on and in it "the miser-merman Wisdom revealed his hoarded heaps" to castaway Pip. "He saw God's foot on the treadle of the loom"—the loom of fate—and bore witness to it. "So man's insanity is heaven's sense; and wandering from all mortal reason, man comes at last to that celestial thought, which, to reason, is absurd and frantic; and weal or woe, feels then uncompromised, indifferent as his God" (1136). In this Pip became a sort of brother to Ahab, except that while Pip testified to an indifferent God, Ahab assumed a malevolent one—the ocean suggesting indifference, the Whale intention. Ahab's God, embodied in the Whale, is Satanic; Pip's more comprehensive embodiment of God, the ocean in which the Whale swims, has proved as indifferent as the human, economic forces and inclinations that combined to cast him into it. In Ishmael's formulation a personal God does control Fate—not the other way around, as the ancient Greeks supposed—but that personal God doesn't much care about His creation.

Stubb killed the whale he abandoned Pip to hunt, and the great corpse needed processing. The whale's sperm crystallizes when exposed to air, so the first thing the sailors did was to squeeze the lumps back into fluid—"a sweet and unctuous duty!" Ishmael exclaims (1238). The first stage of industrial processing, the one closest to nature, where human hands restore the generative part of nature to its original state, provides the human manipulators with short-lived relief from the war of all against all. "I bathed my hands among those soft, gentle globules of infiltrated tissues, woven"—like fate—"almost within the hour." Ishmael could forget "our horrible oath"—the unnatural, polluting oath—to hunt the Whale; so much so, "I almost began to credit the old Paracelsan superstition that sperm is of rare virtue in allaying threat of anger: while bathing in that bath, I felt divinely free from all ill-will, or petulance, or malice, of any sort whatsoever" (1238). This is the natural baptism of the natural religion, producing "a strange sort of insanity" (counterbalancing the ocean-invoked insanity of Pip), and overcoming the condition of isolato-ism: "I found myself squeezing my co-laborers' hands in it, mistaking their hands for the gentle globules," with "an abounding, affectionate, friendly, loving feeling" nearest to the state of grace man experiences in Melville's nature—"the very milk and sperm of kindness" (1239). Would that it would last "for ever!" "For now, since by many prolonged, repeated experiences, I have perceived that in all cases man must eventually lower, or at least shift, his conceit of attainable felicity; not placing it anywhere in the intellect or the fancy; but in the wife, the hearth, the bed, the table, the saddle, the fire-side, the country; now that I have perceived all this, I am ready to squeeze eternally," ready for night-dreams of "long rows of angels in paradise, each with his hands in a jar of spermaceti" (1239). Temporarily at least, Pip's lost *joie de vivre* returned not to him but to his witness during this human analogue to the center of the whales' armada, this social equivalent to the inner Tahiti of the soul, human beings acting in contrast with the indifferent God whose careless foot works the treadle of Fate.

Because business is business, Ishmael describes several other products taken from the dead whale, to be cut up in the "blubber-room" with sharpened spades—the sort of dangerous work that injured Stubb's crewman when extracting ambergris (1240). In yet another parody of churchiness, Ishmael remarks the preliminary 'blessing' of the cutting-up, as the sailors skinned the penis of the whale, dried it on the rigging, then helped one of their mates into it, making him look like a bishop in his "decent black" vestments. He danced on deck. "What a lad for a Pope was this mincer!" (1243).

Modern industrialism proves less than holy, however, as a vision of Hell replaces Ishmael's vision of Heaven. The whale-parts go into the try-pots, heated with "snaky flames." Tended by the "fiend shapes" of "pagan harpooneers" with their "uncivilized laughter," smelling like Hindu funeral pyres, the try-pot spirit pervaded the ship. "The rushing *Pequod*, freighted with savages, and laden with fire, and burning a corpse, and plunging into this blackness of darkness, seemed the material counterpart of her monomaniac commander's soul" (1246). Standing at the helm of the ship, steering it, Ishmael briefly fell asleep, awakening disoriented, somehow having turned around—converted—away from the ship's compass, toward the glowing try-works, no longer "bound to any haven ahead as rushing from all havens astern" with "a stark, bewildered feeling, as of death" (1247). As he regained his bearings, the "unnatural hallucination" ended, but: "Look not too long in the face of the fire, O man! Never dream with thy hand on the helm." Even in daytime, when the sun dispels the perplexing gloom the ocean itself remains, "which is two thirds of this earth." "Therefore, that mortal man who hath more of joy than sorrow in him, that mortal man cannot be true— not true, or undeveloped" (1247). The "truest of all men was the Man of Sorrows," Jesus (1248). The true books of the Bible are Solomon's, made of "the fine hammered steel of woe" that comes from understanding that all is vanity. "This willful world hath not got hold of un-Christian Solomon's wisdom yet," and only "sick men," sufferers like poets William Cowper and Arthur Young, philosophers Pascal and Rousseau, prove true, not "care-free" Rabelais, or Pip before being cast away (1248). Gazing at the fire too long causes a man to wander out of the way of understanding, Solomon teaches, as it brings the wanderer into the congregation of the dead.

Neither Ahab nor Pip, then, bears comprehensive witness: "There is wisdom that is woe; but there is a woe that is madness," a woe that has gazed into the fire, that has been lost in the ocean, too long. In some men, however, "there is a Catskill eagle," a soul "that can alike dive down into the blackest gorges, and soar out of them again and become invisible in the sunny spaces. And even if he for ever flies within the gorge, that gorge is in the mountains; so that even in his lowest swoop the mountain eagle is still higher than other birds upon the plain, even though they soar" (1248). The eagle's soul knows the sorrow of Jesus, the prophet, priest, and king, and the practical wisdom of Solomon, the poet-philosopher-king of Scripture. Nor does such wisdom confine itself to such an eminence, as seen when the sailors take their empty lamps for refilling in the night. "With what genuine freedom the whaleman takes his handful of lamps," fills them with plentiful oil, fresh and genuine because he hunted for it (1249). Merchant sailors live in darkness, trafficking in goods they neither acquire nor produce for themselves. After night falls, whalemen live by the light of a moderate and cheering fire. Human dignity that stays close to nature, yes; industrialism, no. In Young America, the few eagles and the many lamp-men might form an alliance against the excesses of commerce and industry.

If so, the ship of state will be cleansed, at least sometimes. That happens even on the *Pequod*, with its much less wholesome regime. Once the whale has been fully dismembered, its parts processed and stored, the sperm oil cleans the ship, leaving its planks unstained and fragrant. Ishmael never forgets the real, ever-cycling world, though: "Many is the time the poor fellows, just buttoning the necks of their clean frocks, are startled by the cry of 'There she blows!' and away they fly to fight another whale, and go through the whole weary thing again"—a "man-killing" exercise. "Yet this is life." "Old Pythagoras" was right; in this worldly sense at least, life reincarnates itself perpetually (1252).

It is hard to see that cycle because human souls themselves often get in their own way as they attempt to understand the world. Returning to the "horrible oath" the crew swore with Ahab, Ishmael records the soliloquies seven men deliver as they contemplate the doubloon Ahab nailed to the mast. Each 'read' the markings stamped on the doubloon (regarded as "the white whale's talisman") in accordance with the nature of his soul. Ahab saw in it "egotistical mountain-tops and towers," "proud as Lucifer"; he quite self-consciously saw himself; "all" the figures on the doubloon "are Ahab," sailing "from storm to storm!" "So be it, then," he concludes (1154). Starbuck read the doubloon with characteristic pious pessimism; "in this vale of Death, God girds us round, and all over our gloom, the sun of Righteousness still shines a beacon and a hope." But his piety immediately gives way: "Oh, the great sun is no fixture; and if, at midnight, we would fain snatch some sweet solace from him, we gaze for him in vain!" In his genteel, not-quite-Christian decency, he reveals his soul in giving up: "I will quit" gazing at the doubloon, "lest Truth shake me falsely" (1255). Here is how Ishmael learned, as he had announced earlier, that Starbuck could never stand against spiritual terror.

Worldly Stubb saw no suggestions of God in the doubloon but a picture of "the life of man," circling from birth to death like the signs of the Zodiac (1256). Flask saw no meaning in it at all; it is money. The sagacious old Manxman saw it betokening an ill omen. Queequeg silently compared the markings on the coin with the tattoos on his body, finding Sagittarius, he archer, the right image for a harpooner; he finally gave up trying to figure the thing out, knowing that he did not know. As befitted a man who had gazed at the fire too long, Fedallah saw the burning image of the sun on the coin and bowed to his god, the fire. Finally, Pip stepped up, having watched all the others, including Ishmael. He was the true 'reader' or prophet of the doubloon, foreseeing the ship's destruction in its markings. Having discovered the primal sea, he expected it to claim the *Pequod* and its men. Each man saw part of the truth in the doubloon, refracted by his own soul. Socrates-like, it is Ishmael who gathers the speeches of all, presenting the more comprehensive understanding.

To the gam, then—that is, to the dialogue. The *Samuel Enderby* of London bore the name of the founder of a prominent mercantile firm, the first to fit out English wale ships that "regularly hunted the Sperm Whale"— this, only a year before America's Declaration of Independence. (Ishmael hastily adds that the Nantucketers "were the first among mankind to harpoon [the Sperm Whale] with civilized steel" (1266).) The ship's "burly, good-natured" Captain Boomer had lost an arm to Moby-Dick, a fact that induced Ahab to make the unprecedented gesture of boarding a rival ship, despite the difficulty of hoisting him aboard (1259). Unlike Ahab, the English captain thanked God that his arm was nearly severed by the harpoon stuck to the side of the Whale; otherwise, he would have been dragged into the ocean. He preferred an amputated arm to death by drowning and bore the Whale no grudge. The ship physician (a former clergyman) explained that whales can't digest men's arms, anyway: "What you," Ahab, "take for the White Whale's malice is only his awkwardness," as the monster "only thinks to terrify with feints," not to injure (1264). Ahab had none of that. Captain Boomer concluded, "No more White Whales for me. He's best left alone." The commercial-industrial and eminently sane Brits judged Ahab to be mad. As for Ahab, he set his "face like flint"—a man of sorrows, indeed, although more in the mold of an anti-Christ than the Christ who so set His face as he walked off to His Crucifixion.

Ishmael adds a coda to the yarn. "Very long after" this voyage, Ishmael joined another gam on the *Samuel Enderby*, finding it "a jolly ship" with a hospitable crew—"crack fellows all." English sailors are famous for their hospitality. Hollanders, Zealanders, and Danes preceded England in whaling, and their "fat old fashions" included "plenty to eat and drink" on board. "High livers," they stocked their ships with beer, gin, and beef (1268). Although English merchant ships, their owners eyeing the profit margin, scrimp their crews, the whalers imitate their northern European predecessors. "Hence, in the English, this thing of whaling good cheer is not normal and natural, but incidental and particular"—a matter of tradition (1268). They are Burkeans of good cheer, no longer fearing French revolutionaries or mad Tom Paine. Ishmael draws an Epicurean moral: "If you can get nothing better out of the world, get a good dinner out of it" (1270). One might call this the inner Tahiti of the gut; the regime of England enjoys it.

## Chapter Eleven
# IVORY AND STEEL

The next gam will return the *Pequod* and its crew to a glimpse of the American regime in the form of the *Bachelor*, its crew gladly heading back to Nantucket, loaded with sperm oil and intent on partying all the way back. The chapters leading up to this encounter will (to understate the matter) present a contrast to that spirit of festive superficiality.

Ishmael begins by continuing his anatomization of the Sperm Whale, digging down to its "ultimatum," the skeleton. "Since Jonah, few whalemen have penetrated very far beneath he skin of the adult whale," but on a later voyage Ishmael saw a rare, nearly complete skeleton on the island of Tranque (today's Malaita) in the Solomon Islands (1271). Ishmael uses the French name, Arsacides, which means Island of the Assassins; many French and English missionaries have been killed there, and likely eaten, too. No evangelist, Ishmael was safe, having befriended the king, who had collected the skeleton after a whale washed ashore, dead, during a typhoon. He housed it in a temple; the local priests tended it, worshipping it as a god. There is no suggestion that Ishmael's "royal friend" thinks of it as such (1272). The Solomon-Island king has none of the reverence of Solomon, although he may have some of his practical wisdom.

But the skeleton is a god, in its own way. Vines have grown under and through it; "the industrious earth beneath was as a weaver's loom, with a gorgeous carpet on it, whereof the ground-vine tendrils formed the warp and woof, and the living flowers the figures [...]. Through the lacings of the leaves, the great sun seemed a flying shuttle weaving the unwearied verdure" (1272). This recalls the fate-imagery of the loom worked by Queequeg and Ishmael on the *Pequod*'s voyage, but the weaver-god never speaks, and answers no questions. "The weaver-god, he weaves, and by that weaving is he deafened; and only when we escape it shall we hear the thousand voices that speak through it" (1273). Ishmael warns his listeners to be careful, "so far, in all this din of the great world's loom, thy subtlest thinkings may be overheard afar"—the closest readers will come to an explanation of why Ishmael seems to hear not only the speeches of his officers and fellow crewmen, but their whispers and even their thoughts (1273). Somehow, he has escaped the din of the loom, without dying. This Ishmael is an even more thorough exile than his namesake, an observer of the cosmos, outside even while in it—a bit of a philosopher, that way.

The vines and the skeleton: "Life folded Death; Death trellised Life; the grim god wived with youthful Life, and begat him curly-headed glories" (1273). When the priests objected to Ishmael's efforts at obtaining precise measurements of their god like so many priests, they crave infinity in their deity—they fall into disputes among themselves enabling him to complete his works without further disturbance. It is a picture of the effects of religious disputation, and although Ishmael dismisses scientific systems as another form of myth, as always he takes the measure of concrete aspects of ruling bodies—a political scientist if not necessarily a political philosopher, and a 'politic' one, at that, taking advantage of the foolish quarrels among priests. Seventy-two feet long, the skeleton would have stretched some ninety feet when the monster was alive; more than a third of the skeleton consists of the skull and jaw. The skeleton resembled "the embryo hull a great ship new-laid upon the stocks"; hunted and hunter resemble one another, and at times their roles reverse. But the skeleton finally proves a disappointment, as it was "by no means the mold of [the whale's] invested form," covered in life as it is with vast bulks of cartilage, muscle, fat, and spermaceti. "How vain and foolish, then, thought I, for timid untraveled man to try to comprehend aright this wondrous whale, by merely poring over his dead attenuated skeleton, stretched in this peaceful wood. No. Only in the heart of quickest perils; only when within the eddyings of his angry flukes"—no part of the skeleton—"only on the profound unbounded sea, can the full invested whale be truly and livingly found out" (1277). Although the great spine resembles Pompey's Pillar or a Gothic spire—monuments of triumph and of worship, emblems of man reaching to the heavens—"some little cannibal urchins, the priests' children"—had stolen the smaller vertebrae for their games of marbles. "Thus we see how that the spine of even the hugest of living things tapers off at least into simple child's play" (1278). And how children of reverent fathers may think of the gods of their fathers, and perhaps of their fathers.

From the present, Ishmael takes his investigation to the past, the "antediluvian point of view" afforded by examination of whale fossils (1279). In giving this task to his narrator, Melville has him deliver an *apologia* for the novel: "In the mere act of penning my thoughts of this Leviathan, they weary me, and make me faint with their outreaching comprehensiveness of sweep, as if to include the whole circle of the sciences, and all the generations of whales, and men, and mastodons, past, present, and to come, with all the revolving panoramas of empire on earth, and such throughout the whole universe, not excluding its suburbs. Such, and so magnifying, is the virtue of a large and liberal theme! We expand to its bulk. To produce a mighty book, you must choose a mighty theme" (1279–1280). Considering the Flood, for example, returns Ishmael to "Saturn's grey chaos," to the ice ages, when "the whole world was the whale's," then "king of creation"—thus outranking man in Ishmael's unbiblical vision (1281). (And even in Biblical terms, there was a time before Man's creation, in which the whale might indeed have ruled the world.) "I am horror-struck at this antemosaic, unsourced existence of the unspeakable terrors of the whale, which, having been before time, must needs exist after all human ages are over," after man has been dethroned. Comprehensive, indeed: godlike, though quite impersonal.

Past, present, and to what is to come: Ishmael's discussion of the whale looks to the future and dismisses accounts by authorities of the past. Some claim that modern whales are smaller than the ancient species, and that fewer whales exist now than in antiquity. Ishmael denies both claims. The physical evidence suggests that whales are now bigger, despite accounts by Pliny and other ancient writers. Nor are they less numerous; it's harder to hunt whales than it is to hunt the nearly-exterminated American bison. "For all these things, we account the whale immortal in his species, however perishable in his individuality"—immortal as a god, but not as an individual god. The Arsacidian cannibal priests are on to something, but too particular in their worship.

Ahab had incorporated part of an ivory skeleton into his person. Returning to the *Pequod*'s deck from the *Samuel Enderby*, he damaged the leg; it needed replacing. At this point, Ishmael reveals the reason for Ahab's mysterious delay in appearing on-deck in the initial weeks of the voyage. Shortly before sailing from Nantucket, Ahab was found lying on the ground at night, unconscious, his ivory leg displaced and nearly piercing his groin; he was cured of his injury only with "extreme difficulty" (1288). "That direful mishap was at the bottom of his temporary reclusiveness." His small circle of acquaintances on-shore invested this "hinted casualty [...] with terrors, not entirely underived from the land of spirits and of wails," and "conspired [...] to muffle up the knowledge of this thing from others" (1289). Fedallah and the Manilan tigers were equally secretive and not at all so underived; a reader might speculate that they bear some responsibility for the direful mishap. Is Ahab's rumored 'deal with the devil' (suggested by down-to-earth Stubb) the result of what amounts to a physical and spiritual protection racket? Ahab himself thinks of such matters as a great-souled man, perverted, might: "While even the highest earthly felicities ever have a certain unsignifying pettiness lurking in them [...] at bottom, all heart-woes, a mystic significance, and, in some men, an arch-angelic grandeur" derive from "the sourceless primogenitures of the gods," the Saturn-world. "The ineffaceable, sad birth-mark in the brow of man, is but the stamp of sorrow in the signers" (1289). Readers see yet again the affinity of outlook between Ahab and his chronicler, Ishmael, who concludes, "let the unseen, ambiguous synod of the air, or the vindictive princes and potentates of fire, have to do or not with earthly Ahab, yet, in this present matter of his leg, he took plain practical procedures—he called a carpenter" (1290). That sounds very much like one of Ishmael's calling-down-to-earth deflations of metaphysical portents, except that Jesus, the Man of Sorrows (as Ishmael has already recalled) was a carpenter. What manner of man will the ship's carpenter prove?

The carpenter proved omnicompetent in repair work, but also "unhesitatingly expert in all manner of conflicting aptitudes, both useful and capricious"—that is, he undertook projects proposed by the sailors, however odd the jobs might be (1291). In this, he did rather resemble Jesus, the supreme Repairer of any and all who come to Him. But unlike Jesus, this carpenter was a stolid man, "with an old, crutch-like, antediluvian, wheezing humorousness, at one with the general stolidity discernible in the whole visible world," not so much one who respects not persons as an ignorer of them (1292). "He was pure manipulator; his brain, if he ever had one, must have early oozed along into the muscles of his fingers" (1293). If a sort of Creator-Repairer, he resembled the uncaring god of Ishmael's world, not the Bible's with an "unaccountable, cunning life-principle in him; this it was, that kept him a great part of the time soliloquizing, but only like an unreasoning wheel, which also hummingly soliloquizes [...] talking all the time to keep himself awake" (1293). Ishmael's cosmic weaver-god, whether personified or not, parodies the solitary, personal Creator-God and Christ of the Bible.

To make his new leg, Ahab employed both the carpenter and the blacksmith. The blacksmith set to work on the buckle-screw, forged with fire. Ahab approved, observing that fire animated man in the myth of Prometheus. To Ahab, to Fedallah, and to the Manilans, life is fire, and they are would-be spirits of the air, free spirits.

As for the carpenter, Ahab engaged him in dialogue. "I dare say thou callest thyself a good workmanlike workman, eh?" If so, can you drive away my sensation of the 'phantom limb'? "Canst thou not drive that old Adam away?"—as the New Testament testifies of Jesus (1296). The carpenter, stolid maker within a cosmos that answers no questions, merely asked if the 'phantom limb' phenomenon is true. Assuring him that it is, Ahab pressed on: "How dost thou know that some entire, living, thinking thing may not be invisibly and uninterpenetratingly standing precisely where thou now standest; aye, and standing there is thy spite?" In the gospel according to Ahab, the existence of a soul is an unlifted curse: "If I still feel the smart of my crushed leg, though it be now so long dissolved; then, why mayst not thou, carpenter, feel the fiery pains of hell for ever, and without a body? Hah!" (1296) His laugh is sardonic because Ahab seethed at the thought of needing another being—God or neighbor—for redemption. "Oh, Life! Here I am, proud as a Greek god, and yet standing debtor to this blockhead for a bone to stand on! I would be free as air; and I'm down in the whole world's books" (1297). Wealthy, he nonetheless saw that he "owes for the flesh in the tongue I brag with." He wished he could "get a crucible, and [go] into it, and dissolve myself down to one small, compendious vertebra"—a compact, self-sufficient piece of whale-ivory, and thus be a condensed version of the god of the Arsacidians (1297). But would children play dice with him, then, the way some say God plays dice with the universe? Ahab hated Jesus for two things: He hated the God of the Bible because He prevented him from being a fiery air-spirit, free to fly; he hated God also for creating him, thereby placing a debt upon him, preventing his self-sufficiency. The remedies he sought—demonic freedom and a sort of 'crucifixion' that would condense him into a piece of the lifeless, ivory part of the god that is the cosmos, a piece both tiny and "compendious"—flatly contradict themselves, unless crucifixion proves the gateway to liberation (1297). But only the God of the Bible can effect that. Or is it rather that Ahab wants to become like his leg, dead and unfeeling? But that doesn't solve the problem of the phantom limb, the question of the soul.

Ishmael immediately moves to show how Ahab's rebellious-tyrannical soul ruled in his regime. As the ship neared the whale-rich seas near Formosa, the sperm-oil casks stowed in the hull began to leak. When First Mate Starbuck asked the Captain for permission to pull the casks up with heavy-duty block and tackle and repair the damaged ones, Ahab characteristically related it all to himself. "Let it leak! I'm all aleak myself!" (1300) But what will the owners say, Starbuck asked—as he hoped, rhetorically. He provoked a tyrannical riposte: "Thou art always prating to me, Starbuck, about those miserly owners, as if the owners were my conscience. But look ye, the only real owner of anything is its commander; and hark ye, my conscience is this ship's keel." The ship is my Fast-fish, and with it I shall make the Whale my Fast-fish, too. Entreatingly, Starbuck said he wanted the two of them "to understand each other better than hitherto," but the tyrant recurred to force, threatening him with a musket, ordering him back on deck. No coward, Starbuck governed his own temper, got up from the cabin chair "half calmly," and concluded the conversation. "Thou hast outraged, not insulted me, sir; but for that I ask thee not to beware of Starbuck; thou wouldst but laugh; but let Ahab beware of Ahab." Once alone, Ahab noted that brave Starbuck "nevertheless obeys"—remarking, "a most careful bravery, that!" (1300) But he also acknowledged to himself that "there's something there" in the First Mate's admonition. He followed Starbuck on deck, and made an equally telling, double-edged remark to him: "Thou art but too good a fellow, Starbuck" (1301). Relenting, Ahab commanded that the casks be lifted. Ishmael, whose knowledge of men's thoughts seems to come and go, offers two possible explanations for Ahab's reversal: "It may have been a flash of honesty in him; or a mere prudential policy," given the urgency of his own mission and his need to avoid any rebellion on board, however remote that possibility may be.

The sailors excavated cask after cask. Queequeg developed a fever caused by "crawling around amid that dampness and slime" (1303). Near death, he too had a request for the carpenter: to build a canoe, so that his body might be placed in it and set adrift, in the way of warriors' funerals on his native island. He got out of his sickbed long enough to try out the canoe-coffin, which he found satisfactory. Pip hovered nearby, calling himself a coward, Queequeg a general. And if Queequeg reached the Antilles, would he please seek out Pip—who, Pip knew, was lost at sea. But Queequeg wouldn't be going anywhere; he recovered as suddenly as he had fallen ill, claiming that he willed himself to live, having recalled some duty onshore. "Mere sickness could not kill him: nothing but a whale, or a gale, or some violent, ungovernable, unintelligent destroyer of that sort" (1306). The coffin became his sea-chest, which he marked with some figures and drawings with which he'd been tattooed by "a departed prophet and seer on his island, who, by those hieroglyphic marks, had written out on his body a complete theory of the heavens and the earth, and a mystical treatise on the art of attaining truth" in a script Queequeg himself could not read. And so the theory and the treatise alike would perish with him, "unsolved to the last" (1307). Ahab considered him, one morning. Never one to overlook another source of self-torment, he exclaimed, "Oh, devilish tantalization of the gods!"—those beings who reveal their secrets in signs no man can comprehend, beyond the prophet who receives the revelations (1307).

The *Pequod* entered the South Sea, Ishmael's dreamed-of destination. "This mysterious divine Pacific zones the whole world about, makes all coasts bay to it; seems the tide-beating heart of earth" (1308). Pan-like, it also seemed an Arcadia of the water, full of the pleasures of music and nymphs. "But few thoughts of Pan stirred in Ahab's brain" in "that sea in which the hated White Whale must even then be swimming" (1308–1309). He turned again to the blacksmith, with his "patient hammer wielded by a patient arm" (1310). No Biblical echoes in him: It was Hephaestus who made weapons for the Olympians before being flung by Zeus from the heavens into the ocean. The same thing happened to blacksmith Perth. On land he had enjoyed a happy home but met with a double assault from the fates: First, his home was emptied by a burglar whom he "himself did ignorantly conduct" into it. "It was the Bottle Conjuror!"—alcoholic drink, to be sure, but also a reference to a hoax in a London theater in 1749, in which a crowd paid to see a magician place himself into a quart bottle, only to be disappointed (1311). Ahab had wished to perform a similar trick of self-concentration, equally impossible. (Hephaestus, too, suffered a delusion, marrying seductive Aphrodite only to be cuckolded by warlike Ares.) The blacksmith never regained his prosperity; his older brother died, leaving him with crushing additional responsibilities. Eventually, his wife and two of their children also died. "The houseless, familyless old man staggered off a vagabond in crepe" (1311–1312). But like Hephaestus, instead he went to sea: "[T]he all-receptive ocean alluringly spread forth his whole plain of unimaginable, taking terrors, and wonderful new-life adventures" (1312). He is deceived again, this time by the beckoning mermaids, who promise marriage but only after death.

Ahab met Perth's patience with impatience. "How can'st thou endure without being mad?" (1315) But although he could face agonies imposed by the fates and even by himself, even the blacksmith couldn't smooth the creases on the Captain's brow, what Ahab took to be the birth-mark on the brow of man, incised by cruel gods. Perth *could* obey his captain's orders, making him a harpoon out of the hardest steel, the kind used for the nails in the hooves of race horses. Once the harpoon was forged, Ahab insisted on finishing the job himself, as Fedallah gazed at the flame. Ahab had the finished harpoon tempered with the blood of the pagan harpooneers "in the name of the devil" (1315). The pole was hickory, the hardest American hardwood; new tow-line was braided into rope for the harpoon. "This done, pole, iron, and rope—like the Three Fates—remained inseparable, and Ahab moodily stalked away with the weapon," his "delirious" howls mocked by the "wretched laugh" of mocking Pip (1316). Are the Three Fates to doom Moby-Dick, or will they entwine Ahab?

If ivory stands for the dead or perhaps lifeless framework of the cosmos, steel for the lifeless thing that kills life, the gold of the sunset on the peaceful Pacific stands for life, giving the ocean the appearance of a "rolling prairie" full of flowers and tall grasses. "All this mixes with your most mystic mood; so that fact and fancy, half-way meeting, interpenetrate, and form one seamless whole" (1317). "However temporary," the effects of "such soothing scenes" moderated Ahab—the sunlight's "golden keys" opening "his own secret golden treasuries," until "his breath upon them prove[d] but tarnishing." "Would to God these blessed calms would last," Ishmael mused, but, as the weaver-god would have it, "the mingled, mingling threads of life are woven by warp and woof: calms crossed by storms, a storm for every calm" (1318). There is no progress. In this, Ishmael departs from the optimistic historicism of his century and the next. "Where lies the final harbor, whence we unmoor no more?" Nowhere. "Our souls are like those orphans whose unwedded mothers die in bearing them: the secret of our paternity lies in their grave, and we must there to learn it" (1318). As before the other golden thing, the doubloon, Starbuck and Stubb found in the glittering Pacific at sunset a reflection of their own souls. Starbuck piously murmured, "Loveliness unfathomable, as ever lover saw in his young bride's eye!—Tell me not of thy teeth-tiered sharks, and thy kidnapping cannibal ways. Let faith oust fact; let fancy oust memory; I look deep down and do believe" (1318). But one can't really look deep down into water that reflects sunlight. Stubb also stayed on the surface, in his own less meditative way. "I am Stubb, and Stubb has his history; but here Stubb takes oaths that he has always been jolly!"

And so to the gam with the *Bachelor*, her whole crew jolly as Stubb. She was an American ship, out of Nantucket, heading home a "glad ship of good luck," loaded with casks of sperm oil, its crew dancing with Polynesian girls all watched over by their jovial, Pan-like captain, who invited Ahab aboard with glass and bottle aloft (1320). To Ahab's "gritted" query about the White Whale, the 'Pan' happily replied, "No; only heard of him; but don't believe in him at all" (1320). Hoping for some sign of darkness, Ahab asked if he'd lost any men. "Not enough to speak of—two islanders, that's all," 'Pan' blithely replied. If Ahab will but come aboard and join the part, "I'll soon take that black from your brow," that hitherto ineffaceable birth-mark from the gods. Judging him a fool, which in many respects his counterpart surely is, Ahab told him, "Thou art a full ship and homeward bound, thou sayst"—perhaps disaster might yet strike them down—"well, call me an empty ship, and outward bound" (1321). This is the only other "call me" command spoken in the yarn, echoing Ishmael's original. In both cases, they are spoken by a self-understood outcast, and in both cases spoken accurately. "So go thy ways, and I will mine," Ahab bids—his way against the gentle breeze, the *Bachelor's* way with it. Reminded of the home toward which the opposite ship was bound, Ahab took a small vial filled with sand, Nantucket sand, the land on which his young wife awaited him. But unlike his pipe, which he disdainfully pitched into the sea because it gave him pleasure, Ahab didn't empty the vial and throw it away. He did indeed have his humanities.

## Chapter Twelve
# STORM

The *Pequod* caught a forward breeze. A few days after its gam with the *Bachelor* the crew killed four whales, one harpooned by Ahab himself, evidently practicing for the anticipated encounter with his nemesis. He considered the way a Sperm Whale dies, turning its head toward the sun: "He too worships fire; most faithful, broad, baronial vassal of the sun!" The seas, "where to traditions no rocks furnish tablets," "life dies sunwards full of faith," only to be spun around "some other way" after death, toward the "dark Hindoo half of nature" (1322) "In vain, oh whale, dost thou seek intercedings with yon all-quickening sun, that only calls forth life, but gives it not again;" Ahabian 'Hinduism' includes no hopeful doctrine of reincarnation (1323). "Yet dost thou, darker half, rock me with a prouder, if a darker faith." Ahab wants nothing of the solid rock of Christ, the Son, turning instead to the larger, darker sea, whose billows "are my foster-brothers" (1323). He seeks a rock in something vast and fluid, a chaos-rock.

One of the whales couldn't be hauled in immediately, so Ahab and his boat-crew stayed with it. Fedallah watched his fellow-predators, the sharks; Ahab told him of a recurring dream, a dream of hearses. It is time for prophecy. Fedallah reminded him that "neither hearse nor coffin can be thine"; at sea, there are no hearses, but before Ahab can die, he must see two hearses at sea, "the first not made by mortal hands," the second made with wood grown in America (1324). What is more, Fedallah must die before Ahab; he must be Ahab's "pilot," his guide into death, if he is to die. In exchange, Fedallah has made two promises: that Ahab shall kill Moby-Dick and survive the killing. Fedallah adds another promise: "[H]emp only can kill thee" (1325). Ahab assumes that Fedallah means death by hanging on the gallows, but should recall that the dangerous, snake-like ropes in the boat he sits in whip dangerously after the harpooner lances a whale. Does Fedallah lie, or deceive?

In the Sea of Japan, land of the rising sun, the summer sea under that sun shimmers with an "unrelieved radiance" like "the insufferable splendors of God's throne," the white throne of judgment (1326). Fire-worshipping Fedallah gazed at the sun, which Ahab (now changing symbols, so to speak) calls "my Pilot." He asked the sun, "Where is Moby-Dick?" (1327) Indeed the sun 'sees' half the world at a time. But the sun, silent as always, told him nothing. In fury he destroyed the ship's quadrant, cursing "Science" and the "foolish toy" devised by scientists; "no longer will I guide my earthly way by thee," not because the quadrant is a human instrument but because it "feebly pointest on high," toward heavenly bodies like the sun, whereas the ship's other instruments, the compass and the log-and-line, point him along the surface of the sea, his fluid rock (1327). Overhearing the Captain's tirade, bluff Stubb concurs. "Damn me, Ahab, but thou actest right; live in the game, and die in it!" (1328) Ishmael isn't Ahab's only secret sharer.

The sea's potential chaos then realized itself. A sudden typhoon struck the *Pequod*. Dutiful Starbuck wished they would ride with the gale, towards home, instead of against it, towards Moby-Dick. Ahab had other plans. As lightning sets fire to the three masts, he shrieks to the crew, "The white flame but lights the way to the White Whale!" Ishmael compares the lightning to "God's burning fingers" as God wrote the words of judgment against Belshazzar, as recounted in the Book of Daniel: "MENE, MENE, TEKEL, UPHARSIN." In that book, the king calls upon the Chaldeans—Fedallah's ancestors—to interpret these words, but they fail. They prove poor prophets. Only Daniel can understand truly: God has numbered the days of Belshazzar's kingdom; the king has been weighed in the balance and found wanting; his kingdom will be divided and given to the Medes and the Persians. Belshazzar is killed the following night. As the 'H' in "UP-HARSIN" implies, the sundering of Ahab's regime will take breath away.

Nevertheless, Ahab followed the Parsee. He prayed to the "trinity of flames," worshipping them in a reversal of the way a Christian would pray to the Holy Trinity: "O! thou clear spirit of clear fire, whom on these seas I as Persian once did worship"—he veers into the doctrine of reincarnation he'd earlier rejected—"till in the sacramental act so burned by thee, that to this hour I bear the scar; I now know thee, thou clear spirit, and I now know that thy right worship is defiance" (1333). There is no kindness in chaos-nature, only "speechless, placeless power." Therefore, "To the last gasp of my earthquake life [I] will dispute its unconditional, unintegral mastery in me. In the midst of the personified impersonal, a personality stands here" (1333). "A true child of fire, I breathe it back to thee" (1334). Months before, Stubb had whispered about Ahab's scar, comparing it to the crack in a tree struck by lightning. If Ahab were an ordinarily evil man, he would lack the nobility he shows here. When lightning strikes a tree and makes a vertical crack in it, it doesn't kill the tree immediately. But the tree will die. The lightning has given the tree a fatal flaw. Ishmael considers Ahab a tragic hero, a thought he reinforces by his periodic allusions to Lear—here, to Ahab's "beaten brain," both comparable with and contrasting with the live, "beating" brain of Shakespeare's king. Ahab's brain has been beaten by its own inner flaw. He had that flaw before he met Fedallah. Did Fate give it to him, or did he give it to himself?

Ahab regarded the Creator-God as mindless. "Thou knowest not how came ye, hence callest thyself unbegotten; certainly knowest not thy beginning, hence callest thyself unbegun [...]. I know that of me, which thou knowest not of thyself, oh, thou omnipotent. There is some unsuffusing thing beyond thee, thou clear spirit, to whom all thy eternity is but time, all thy creativeness mechanical" (1334). For Ahab, as humans are to the God of the Bible, so the Biblical God is to—call it Fate. As a personality confronting an impersonal foolishly supposed personal by mythologizing prophets and priests, and their dupes, Ahab worshipped the truly impersonal, ever-changing Heraclitean Fire by defying it. Prudence dictates otherwise, but why would a *noble* man not defy such a being?

Poor Starbuck read matters differently. When lightning struck Ahab's steel harpoon with "forked fire" like "a serpent's tongue," he told the Captain that "God, God is against thee." Turn home "while we may," he implores, on "a better voyage than this" (1335). This panicked the crew, who "raised a half mutinous cry." Immediately recognizing a nascent revolutionary moment, Ahab seized his burning harpoon and "waved it like a torch among them; swearing to transfix with it the first sailor that but cast loose a rope's end"—the rope of hemp, the one thing that might kill him. This threat of force stopped them, giving him a chance to reinforce his rule with speech, reminding them of their oath to hunt the White Whale, an oath "as binding as mine"—'totalitarian,' encompassing "heart, soul, and body, lungs and life." To these words he added a final action, blowing out the fire on the harpoon and roaring, "Thus I blow out the last fear!" (1335) The last fear of God (in Biblical terms, the last hope for the beginning of wisdom) will not be the last fear in the souls of his men. Quite the contrary: Instead of overpowering the tyrant, the men, so threatened and so reminded, fled in terror. Starbuck's words, which might have rallied 'the many' to his side, had failed.

"Oh, none but cowards send down their brain trucks in tempest time," Ahab said to himself, even as he reminded himself, Lear-like, to "take medicine" (1336). But while Lear takes "physic" in order to expose himself "to feel what wretches feel" and thus dispose himself to charity toward them, Ahab remains a tyrant, not a king, knowing what wretches feel only to rule them for his own purpose, not their succor. As for the officers and the harpooneers, they do not share in the sailors' panic but neither do their souls have the strength to rebel; Stubb could only say to Flask, "This is a nasty night, lad," and Tashtego wished for a glass of rum (1338). At his moment, was anyone on the *Pequod* better than a would-be drunken Indian?

The typhoon passed, the crew cheered and began repairing the ship, as ordered by the officers. The 'many' respond to immediate success and failure; except for Starbuck, the 'few'—officers and harpooneers—were little better. Only the First Mate clearly saw the ultimate disaster to which Ahab directed the ship. Only he could act to stop it, and chance now gave him the opportunity.

Starbuck went below deck to report to his Captain on the new conditions on deck. He saw the muskets in the gun rack, including the musket Ahab had aimed at him. "An evil thought" occurred to him, which he found hard to suppress (1341). Should he kill Ahab, as Ahab had been ready to kill him? The gun was already loaded.

How evil is that thought? "Shall this crazed old man be tamely suffered to drag a whole ship's company down to doom with him"—effectively murdering more than thirty men in his willful, sustained act of tyrannical usurpation? (1341) Starbuck found Ahab asleep, incapable of resisting. Neither reasoning, nor remonstrance, nor entreaty had swayed the tyrant; Starbuck had tried them all. *Alogos*, immoralist, and un-agapic, the tyrant demanded only "flat obedience to [his] own flat commands." As for the vow, the contract Ahab had cited, "Great God forbid!" that we make ourselves lesser Ahabs (1342). Ahab's real underlying 'contract,' the one with

Fedallah, ignores the good of the ship and crew; a king would rule for the god of his people but the tyrant rules for himself, for an illusory self-interest. Assenting to the contract with Ahab, officers, harpooneers, and crew assented to the contract with Fedallah, a soul reminiscent of the Prince of Liars.

Was there no "lawful way" to proceed? No: Restrained, Ahab "would be more hideous than a caged tiger, then, I could not endure the sigh; could not possibly fly his howlings; all comfort, sleep itself, inestimable reason would leave me on the long intolerable voyage" (1342). Ahab would murder sleep, as Macbeth's conscience did; an anti-conscience, Ahab was the monster that would put reason to sleep. There was no law for Starbuck to fear, here on the open sea. "Is heaven a murderer when its lightning strikes a would-be murderer, tindering sheets and skin together?" (1342) Surely not: Starbuck might kill with impunity and also without moral hazard. With Ahab dead, Starbuck might then return home to his own wife— named Mary, for the mother of Jesus—and their child, again. Without Ahab dead, he would not. Personal, political, and familial morality alike command tyrannicide.

Starbuck the appealed to the final authority. "Great God, where art thou? Shall I? shall I?" (1342) Nowhere in this yarn does God speak to anyone. Events occur, which may or may not be interpreted as providential, but God is always silent. Here, only Ahab spoke, in his unreasoning sleep. After Starbuck made his brief report to the Captain, Ahab in his dream replied, characteristically, with a command: "Stern all! Oh, Moby-Dick, I clutch thy heart at last!" It was "as if Starbuck's voice," as he softly dialogued with himself and his God, and then with Ahab, "had caused the long dumb dream to speak." "Starbuck seemed wrestling with an angel." Unlike Jacob, he let go. "He placed the death-tube in its rack, and left the place" (1342). He went back on deck and told Stubb to wake Ahab and make the report, prevaricating that "I must see to the deck here" (1343). His conscience had made a coward of him. There would be no just *coup d'état*, no revolution against tyranny on the *Pequod*. The ship's ruler pursued defiant rebellion against the personified impersonal and, more mundanely, against the owners of the ship; its potential ruler could not bring himself to rebel against that ruler. These two extremes spell catastrophe as surely as MENE, MENE, TEKEL, UPHARSIN.

In the aftermath of the natural storm and the political near-storm, the waves still billowed, the sunlight gleaming on the ocean, making it seem "a crucible of molten gold." Refreshed after his nap, Ahab exclaimed in megalomaniacal exultation, "All ye nations before my prow, I bring the sun to ye!" (1244) As Melville's symbolism would have it, the ship's compass needle had been deranged by the lightning strike, so Ahab took charge of adjusting the ship's course. Officers and men obeyed; "though some of [the sailors] lowly rumbled, their fear of Ahab was greater than their fear of Fate"— likely not the wiser fear (1245). As for the "pagan harpooneers," they remained imperturbable; "if impressed, it was only with a certain magnetism shot into their congenial hearts from inflexible Ahab's." Ahab had replaced the compass of the ship and the sailors, both. As for the tyrant himself, he proclaimed himself "lord of the level loadstone," overawing "the superstitious sailors" by making a new compass and gesticulating mysteriously over it, as if commanding it to come to life. Having regretfully rejected the human home, the earth, the sands of Nantucket; having defiantly rejected the heavenly God, dashing the quadrant, Ahab claimed mastery over men by controlling power of navigation over the chaos-sea. "In his fiery eyes of scorn and triumph, you then saw Ahab in all his fatal pride" (1347).

The compass became the first of three new instruments Ahab commanded to be made. The second was the log-and-line. As the compass registers direction, the log-and-line registers the velocity of the ship: The line winds around a reel; a piece of wood, the "log," is tied to the end of the line and is thrown overboard; sailors can then measure the speed at which the ship moves by the length of line pulled from the reel in a given segment of time. The old log-and-line had been damaged by long exposure to the elements; deployed, it snapped. The old Manxman remarked, "To me, the skewer seems loosening out of the middle of the world," but Ahab simply commanded that a new device be made, having concluded from conversing with "the man from Man" that he had no wisdom to offer Ahab, that "the dead, blind wall butts all inquiring heads at last" (1349). When Pip appeared, seeing in the loss of the "log" a picture of his own casting-away, the Manxman would have dismissed him, but Ahab intervened and put him under his protection. To Ahab, deranged Pip fell from the "frozen heavens" and therefore "touchest my inmost centre." Not the sagacious old man but Pip told the true tale, the tale told by an idiot. "Lo! ye believers in gods all goodness, and in man all ill, lo you! see the omniscient gods oblivious to suffering man; and man, though idiotic, and knowing not what he does, yet full of the sweet things of love and gratitude. Come! I feel prouder leading thee by thy black hand, than though I grasped an Emperor's!" (1350) The Manxman judged them "One daft with strength, the other daft with weakness"—true enough, but not comprehensive (1350–1351). Nor do recent scholars who find in this a stinging critique of American slavery quite see the point. The tyrant has his humanities, but they rule his conduct only when considering a soul that seems to him to mirror his own soul, with its own obsessions. Ahab made Pip his missing leg because Pip was crushed by unknowing, unspeaking 'gods.'

Steering the ship by his new compass and measuring its speed by his new log-and-line, Ahab set his course toward the equator, the surface-center of the world. At night the sailors heard a cry sounding "like the half-articulated wailings of the ghosts of all Herod's murdered innocents" (1352). Only the Captain knew what it was: the cries of mother seals that have lost their cubs. In the New Testament, Herod's mass murder, a futile attempt to kill the infant Jesus, recalls Jeremiah's story of Rachel, weeping for her exiled 'children'—her descendants, to be banished to Babylon by God in punishment for their idolatry. As God promises to redeem the guilty Israelites from their exile, so will His Son redeem guilty humanity, which sins repeatedly against Him. The next gam will be a ship called the *Rachel.*

The sailors, however, superstitiously took the seal-cries to signify the cries of lost, drowned sailors. Confirming their forebodings, the next day a man fell from the mast-head and drowned in the sea: "Thus the first man of the *Pequod* that mounted the mast to look out for the White Whale, on the White Whale's own peculiar ground; that man was swallowed in the deep" (1353). The sailors dropped the life-buoy for him, but it too, like the log-and-line, proved too weathered to work; it sank, following the man. Queequeg offered his coffin as a replacement. Starbuck fretted over the symbolism of substituting a coffin for a life-buoy; Flask considers the matter materially; Ahab turns again to the carpenter to reshape the coffin for the new use.

The carpenter again revealed himself as a Jesus according to Ahab, fashioning a means of salvation without knowing what he was doing. To Ahab's accusation, "Thou art as unprincipled as the gods, and as much a jack-of-all-trades," the carpenter could only reply, "But I do not mean anything, sir. I do as I do" (1356). If the Creator-God of the Bible is what He is, willingly shall be what He shall be, the carpenter-god here only does, humbly but mindlessly and will-lessly. Against such a being, Ahab asserted personality—mind and will. "What things real are there, but imponderable thoughts?" "A life-buoy of a coffin!" The coffin, symbol of death, "by a mere hap, made the expressive sign of the help and hope of most endangered life" (1357). Could this have "some spiritual sense" as "an immortality-preserver"? But as soon as Ahab promised himself to "think on that" he exercises his will to deny it. "So far gone am I in the dark side of earth, that its other side, the theoretic bright one, seems by uncertain twilight to me" (1357). He turned not to Christ but to Pip: "We'll talk this over; I do suck most wondrous philosophies from thee!" (1358) His dialogue will not be with Christ, nor even with Socrates, but with a supposed mirror of himself, self-willed agent of will-less *alogos*. Ahab is the supreme isolato of *Moby-Dick*.

## Chapter Thirteen
# END OF THE YARN

As Ahab drew nearer the White Whale, two gams followed in quick succession. New England's Puritan founders had modeled their regimes on the laws of Israel; the name of the first ship recalls the early generations of Israel. The captain of the *Rachel* had not only seen Moby-Dick, he had chased him, losing a boat and a crew to him. The captain's twelve-year-old son was on that boat. The Manxman now took the cries of the seals on the rocks to have been the cries of those drowned sailors. As in the Bible, the *Rachel* mourned her lost sons. Rachel's husband was Jacob; Starbuck had just failed to be a 'Jacob.' Now, he sought no ally in the visiting captain, nor does Ishmael suggest that he so much as thought of doing so. Starbuck was no founder, lacking the strength to follow his God, or to break the human law by committing a founding crime.

The captain of the *Rachel* knew Ahab from Nantucket, knew that Ahab himself had a young son. He implored Ahab to join him in the search, offering to pay for time lost. Ahab refused, with one of his most striking utterances: "May I forgive myself" (1362). Ahab treated himself as God; after all, according to his gospel, he had personality, the ability to judge and forgive, whereas his 'god' had none.

Ishmael explicitly likens the *Rachel* to the Biblical Rachel, the mother of the Jewish people. When Rachel weeps for her future descendants, exiled, God promises to end that exile in His own time, showing mercy for His chosen people. In the Book of Matthew Rachel's story is said to have foreshadowed the murder of innocent children by Herod in his attempt to kill Jesus, prophesied to be a threat to his rule; the life and redemptive crucifixion of Jesus reveals God's mercy not only toward Israelites but toward all peoples. Even as he treats himself as God, Ahab put himself on the side of Herod.

Nonetheless, Ahab continued to have his humanities. Having sent the grieving captain on his way, he returned to his cabin and to Pip, his adopted 'son.' "Lad, lad, I tell thee thou must not follow Ahab now"—not, to be sure, to save Pip from harm but because Pip, like the captain and his son, could distract him from his mission. "There is in thee, poor lad, which I feel too curing to my malady. Like cures like; and for this hunt, my malady becomes my most desired health" (1363). Compassion, *agape*, would impede that hunt. Ahab's sympathy for Pip based itself on the assumption that Pip's imbecility both came from and symbolized the cold indifference of the chaos-cosmos. But Ahab was now proved mistaken. Pip retained a core not only of sanity but of gratitude and compassion in his own soul: "No, no, no! ye have not a whole body sir; do ye but use poor me for your one lost leg; only tread upon me, sir; I ask no more, so I remain a part of ye," the one who adopted him. Pip wept and pled, but as with Starbuck so with Pip: Ahab replied, "Weep so, and I will murder thee!" Ahab then recalled a shred of his Quaker Christianity, relenting only so much as to say, "God for ever bless thee; and if it come to that,—God forever save thee, let what will befall" (1363). That won't happen. By rejecting his many opportunities to change his course, his regime or 'way,' Ahab doomed Pip along with himself. Ishmael comments, "All his successive meetings with various ships contrastingly concurred to show the demoniac indifference with which the white whale tore his hunters, whether sinning or sinned against," but the *telos* of the Ahab regime "domineered above" the "gloomy crew" (1365).[9]

Ahab himself remained in a bondage of his own choosing. "Even as Ahab's eyes so awed the crew's, the inscrutable Parsee's glance awed his; or somehow, at least in some wild way, at times affected it" (1365). Both men stood on deck, day and night, awaiting the appearance of the Whale while gazing at each other, "as if in the Parsee Ahab saw his forethrown shadow, in Ahab the Parsee his abandoned substance"; "both seemed yoked together, and an unseen tyrant driving them" (1367). If so, the question of the *Pequod's* true regime is settled: No human personality rules the ship; its apparent ruler has proudly claimed to stand as a personality against the impersonal while ruling by means of the impersonal all along, unbeknownst to himself.

9    For a comparison of Ahab and Pip with King Lear and his fool, see Olson, op. cit., 58–63.

Distrusting the dispirited crew, suspecting that they might deliberately pretend not to sight the Whale, Ahab commanded that he be hoisted to the top of a mast to serve as lookout. He shrewdly trusted Starbuck to hold the rope that hoisted him up, rightly convinced that the First Mate would not allow an 'accident' to befall him. It would have been easy for Starbuck to arrange such a thing, but his God remains as silent as Ahab (or Machiavelli) would expect.

If God does not speak in words, does He nonetheless speak in actions? As Ahab perched on the mask, a "sea-eagle" seized his hat and carried it away, dropping it into the sea. Ishmael recalls an omen associated with another intruder-usurper, Tarquin, the fifth king of ancient Rome. "An eagle flew thrice around Tarquin's head, removing his cap to replace it, and thereupon Tanaquil, his wife"—reputed a prophetess—"declared that Tarquin would be king of Rome." "But only by the replacing of the cap," Ishmael recalls, "was that omen counted good. Ahab's hat was never restored" (1368–1369). Regime change is indeed 'in the air,' now.

In ancient philosophy, Roman or Greek, the right *telos* of man and regimes was *eudaimonia* or the happiness attendant to the full development of human nature. Fedallah was no good *daimon*, Machiavelli no good philosopher, Ahab no good man. In its final gam the *Pequod* met the teleologically-named and, given its circumstances "most miserably named" *Delight*. Moby-Dick had shattered one of its boats, killing five men; captain and crew were burying, with prayer, the only body they had recovered. After hearing this, Ahab "like lightning" ordered his ship to sail on; his crew must not be permitted to dwell upon death, or God, lest fear of either overcome their fear of their ruler. Ahab imitated the god he has adopted, the electric fire which had caused his harpoon to burn with the fire of a serpent's tongue, terrifying the murmuring crew into obedience.

The tyrant himself had nearly reached the end of the rope of his will. If thoughts of his moral and political responsibilities, his family, and the Biblical God had not deterred him, could natural sentiments reach him? Ishmael describes the "symphony" of nature on the Pacific, as the "feminine" air, "transparently pure and soft," and the "masculine" sea, with its "strong, troubled, murderous thinkings" blended into an "all-pervading azure" of "a clear steel-blue day." For a while, "those two seemed one," as the sun "seemed giving his gentle air to his bold and rolling sea; even as bride to groom"—a natural parallel to the spiritual doctrine of 'one flesh' or, alternatively, to a Hegelian synthesis of opposites (1372). Ahab responded. "The step-mother world, so long cruel—forbidding—now threw affectionate arms around his stubborn neck, and did seem to joyously sob over him, as if over one, that however willful and erring, she could yet find it in her heart to save and bless" (1373). Nature might 'save' the man the Biblical God does not save—save him at least from tyrannical ambition and folly. "Ahab dropped a tear into the sea; nor did all the Pacific contain such wealth as that one wee drop" (1373). This is the humane counterpart to Ahab's proud defiance of the personified impersonal. He will not let himself be ruled by the sentiment.

Starbuck approached him, and Ahab offers the most pious man on his ship what amounts to a confession, calling himself a fool, an "Adam, staggering beneath the piled centuries since Paradise." "Starbuck, let me look into a human eye; it is better than to gaze into sea or sky; better than to gaze upon God. By the green land; by the bright hearth-stone! this is the magic glass, man; I see my wife and child in thine eye" (1374). He told Starbuck to stay on board the ship when the whale boats next lower for Moby-Dick.

At this moment, Starbuck's decision not to kill his captain seemed good. Better than dying a tyrant, Ahab might have returned if not to Christianity then at least to natural moral sentiment, to filial devotion to hearth and home—what Aristotle considered the foundation of political life. Starbuck urged Ahab to change course. "I think, sir, they have some such mild blue days, even as this, in Nantucket" (1374). "But Ahab's glance was averted" from his First Mate's human eye; "like a blighted fruit tree," Eden's Tree of Knowledge, "he shook, and cast his last, cindered apple to the soil," rejecting what he acknowledged as "all natural lovings and longings" of "my own natural heart," recurring to the "handspike" of "Fate" (1375). Not the natural-right philosophy of Aristotle, or even the natural-rights philosophy of Rousseau but the fatalism of the Greek tragedians (and of Nietzsche, after Melville) remained Ahab's North Star to the last. He *chose* "Fate," showing that fatalism is fatal*ism*. Starbuck left in despair; Ahab caught Fedallah's eyes, reflected on the water When Moby-Dick reappeared the next day, captain and crew returned to the hunt.

The Whale "divinely swam" with "a gentle joyousness," like a Jupiter or Jove of the sea (1379). Nature *turns* hostile but need not always be so.

Knowing his own fate, Fedallah watched Moby-Dick with "a pale, death-glimmer" in "his sunken eyes; a hideous motion gnawed his moth," anticipating he same motion taken by the Whale's jaw, which soon crushed Ahab's boat and Fedallah and his 'tigers' in it. The ship rescued Ahab and crew, and here Ishmael pays tribute to the Captain's greatness. Battered and exhausted, "nameless wails came from him, as desolate sounds from out ravines." "In an instant's compass, great hearts sometimes condense into one deep pang, the sum total of those shallow pains kindly diffused through feebler men's whole lives." "Such hearts" might, "in their life-time aggregate a whole age of woe, wholly made up on instantaneous intensities; for even in their pointless centres, those noble natures contain the entire circumferences of inferior souls" (1383). Ishmael's language recalls the virtue he saw in Jesus, that He was a man of sorrows; if Ahab amounted to an anti-Christ, he was at least an anti-*Christ*, no Starbuck and very far from a Stubb.

Recovering quickly, Ahab ascertained that no men had been lost and ordered the boat to be repaired. Materialist Stubb joked at the ruined boat (garbling an Aesop fable as he did), earning the Captain's rebuke: "What soulless thing is this that laughs before a wreck?" (1385) For his part, Starbuck saw an ill omen in it, drawing a still sharper scolding: "Omen? omen?—the dictionary! If the gods think to speak outright to man, they will honorably speak outright; not shake their heads, and give an old wives' darkling hint" (1385). His riposte must have hit Starbuck harder than Ahab knew, as God had indeed failed to answer Starbuck's plea for guidance when he considered committing tyrannicide. "Begone! Ye two are opposite poles of one thing [...] and ye two are all mankind; and Ahab stands alone among the millions of the peopled earth, nor gods nor men his neighbors!" (1385) He would be the greatest isolato of all, the supreme, all-ruling tyrant. As such, he moved again to secure his rule, announcing that the doubloon will go to the man who sights the Whale on the day it's killed, then assuring his men that if he the one to seem him first, he'll pay each man ten times the value of the doubloon. This lifted the gloom that had threatened to undermine his rule.

On the second day of the hunt, newly-motivated Stubb exuberantly predicted that Ahab would kill Moby-Dick; he "did but speak out for well nigh all that crew." "The hand of Fate had snatched all their souls; and by the stirring perils of the previous day; the rack of the past night's suspense;

the fixed, unfearing, blind, reckless way in which their wild craft went plunging towards its flying mark; by all these things, their hearts were bowled along" by the no-longer gentle wind, which "seemed the symbol of that unseen agency which so enslaved them to the race" (1388–1389). They had become fast-fish, not loose-fish. They had achieved perfect unity: "All varieties were welded into oneness, and were directed to that fatal goal which Ahab their one lord and keel did point to," striving "through that infinite blueness to seek out the thing that might destroy them" (1389). Like Ahab's harpoon, the tyrant-forged unity of the regime cut through the evanescent but natural unity of peaceful air, sea, and sunshine. Indeed, the rising wind now "rushed the vessel on by arms invisible as irresistible" (1389). Unlike the American regime, intended to keep the many varieties of citizens checked from their worst passions by setting ambition against ambition, interest against interest, thereby achieving a dynamic balance, Ahab's crew now fused themselves to one will and one fate.

At the next lowering, Moby-Dick smashed two of the boats, not before entangling them in their own harpoon lines, like the weaver-god, Fate. He then attacked Ahab's boat from below, and Ahab's ivory leg splintered off. Rescued a second time, Ahab remained defiant: "Nor white whale nor man, nor fiend, can so much as graze old Ahab in his own proper and inaccessible being," which is no inner Tahiti (1393). But Fedallah had disappeared, dragged under by Ahab's line; given the prophecy Fedallah had issued and Ahab had believed, this gave the Captain pause. Starbuck took the event for one final chance at dissuasion: "They evil shadow gone—all good angels mobbing thee with warnings:—what more wouldst thou have? [...]. Oh, oh,—impiety and blasphemy to hunt him more!" (1394) But to him who denies the personal God, there can be no blasphemy except in the failure to resist, while contradictorily claiming fidelity to the chaos-cosmos. "Fool! I am the Fates' lieutenant; I act under orders" (1394). This time, he had it right. Turning to the superstitious sailors, he took care to sever any connection between Starbuck's appeal and their beliefs. "Believe ye, men, in the things called omens? Then laugh aloud, and cry encore! For ere they drown, drowning things will twice rise to the surface; then rise again, to sink for evermore. So with Moby-Dick [...]" (1394). But of course the same 'omen' might as well apply to the Captain himself. The supreme isolato, the ruler of supreme self-will, lacks self-knowledge. Speaking to himself, Ahab saw one of his contradictions, a different and deeper one: "Oh! how valiantly I seek to drive out of others' hearts what's clenched so fast in mine!"—namely, the Parsee's omen or prophecy that he would "go before" Ahab in death, yet must be "seen again ere I could perish." He vowed to solve this "riddle," and would do so, on the third day of the hunt.

His ivory leg replaced by the carpenter's latest, last efforts, Ahab observed the beauty of the third day, calling it "food for thought, had Ahab time to think; but Ahab never thinks, he only feels, feels, feels; *that's* tingling enough for mortal man!" "God only has that right and privilege, the right and privilege to think. (1396) Willfully thoughtless Ahab then thought, speaking a monologue to the wind. It is "a coward wind that strikes stark naked men, but will not stand to receive a single blow. Even Ahab is a braver thing—a nobler thing that *that*. Would now that the wind but had a body; but all the things that most exasperate an outrage mortal man, all these things are bodiless, but only bodiless as objects, not as agent. There's a most special, a most cunning, oh, a most malicious difference!" (1397) The wind can strike but not be struck in retaliation. The wind is like God, a spirit, exasperating but at times "glorious and gracious" (1397). For the moment, Ahab's mind swayed, so to speak, in the wind. But Moby-Dick's reappearance tore him out of his thoughtful, willed thoughtlessness. This time, not only Ahab but the men on the three mastheads sighted the Whale simultaneously. "Three shrieks went up" from the sailors "as if tongues of fire had voiced it." Fedallah's spirit was now in the crew, talking in tongues inspired by an unholy spirit.

As for the Whale, the spirit of fire had risen in him, as well. "Maddened by yesterday's fresh irons that corroded in him, Moby-Dick seemed combinedly possessed by all the angels that fell from heaven" (1401). Upon sighting him, Ahab had bravely denied that Fedallah's prophecy of doom could come true—that Ahab would die after seeing Fedallah one last time. How could a crowned man be seen again? "Aye, aye, like many more thou told'st direful truth as touching thyself, O Parsee; but Ahab, there thy shot fell short" (1398). "What is more, he exulted, "no coffin and no hearse can be mine—only hemp can kill me!" (1400)

Moby-Dick surfaced, breaching the waves once again with a majestic, warning leap into the air. Pinioned to the Whale's body by harpoon ropes, Fedallah's body reappeared with the monster, the Parsee's "distended eyes turned full upon old Ahab" (1401). The Captain dropped his harpoon, seeing the prophecy fulfilled: Moby-Dick himself was the hearse. But "where is the second hearse?" Ahab demanded, threatening his boat-mates with harpooning if they jumped off their craft. "Ye are not other men, but my arms and my legs; and so obey me" (1402). As the Whale began to swim off, Starbuck watched from the deck of the *Pequod*, saying, "See! Moby-Dick seeks thee not. It is thou, thou, that madly seekest him!" (1402)

True enough, but when Ahab ordered Starbuck to set the *Pequod*'s sails to follow his whale-boat, Starbuck again obeyed. The three harpooneers mounted the masts; while Ahab had chased the Whale, a sea-eagle had carried off the ship's red flag; when Ahab saw it was no longer on the mainmast, he ordered Tashtego to replace it. Ahab's boat caught up with Moby-Dick, and when Ahab's re-seized harpoon struck the Whale, Moby-Dick charged not the boat but the now-nearby ship itself, "smiting his jaws amid fiery showers of foam" (1404). Fiery showers: fire and water, Ahab's worshiped "Father" and "Step-Mother," combine in one image. "Is this the end of all my bursting prayers? all my lifelong fidelities?" panicked Starbuck wondered. The answer is yes, as Moby-Dick, "retribution, swift vengeance, eternal malice […] in his whole aspect," "smote the ship's starboard bow," breaching it with "his predestinating head" (1405). Ahab saw and understood: The ship was the second hearse, the one made of American wood.

Ahab made one last throw with the harpoon of the satanic baptism. This time the snaking hemp rope caught him, pulling him from the boat into the sea. The ship sank, sucking the last boat into its whirlpool. Tashtego, representative of the 'first' Americans, at the top of the mainmast, was the last to go down on the American-made hearse. Just before he did, he pinned the swooping sea-eagle to the mast, as it attempted to fly off with the replacement flag. Having carried off Ahab's hat and the first flag on his ship, the sea-eagle dies in its third attempt. Thus, Ishmael thinks, the ship was like Satan, who took a part of Heaven to Hell along with him. Clean of the ship and its boats, "The great shroud of the sea rolled on as it rolled five thousand years ago"—the time of the Flood (1407). The grand "moving land," Leviathan, mortally wounded the ship; the forces of the air had decrowned its tyrant but were killed by the First American, himself killed in the all-consuming chaos-cosmos of water along with all but one of the crew of the ship named for First Americans.

"And I only am escaped alone to tell thee" (1408). The Epilogue's epigram is from Job 1: 14–19, the coda of each of the four messengers who reported a flood of disasters to Job. Ishmael means to be the bringer of bad news to Americans. But why? He is, after all, an Ishmael, a perpetual exile.

He had been thrown overboard from Ahab's whale-boat during the fight. He ascribes his presence in Ahab's boat to "the Fates," who caused him to take the place of Fedallah there. Thrown from the boat, "floating on the margin of the ensuring scene, and in full sight of it"—exiled by Moby-Dick, Fate's agent—he found himself slowly drawn "towards the closing vortex" as the *Pequod* sank. "Like another Ixion did I revolve" (1408). Ixion is the Ishmael-figure of classical mythology, equally an exile, although for the crime of having pushed his father into a fire. The gods took him up, much to their regret, and eventually his adultery with Hera provoked Jupiter to attach him to a wheel of fire for eternity. The physical wheel of water has its counterpart in the mythological wheel of fire, as both these contradictory elements served as objects of Ahabian worship. Unlike Ixion, or Ahab, Ishmael escaped the wheel. Queequeg's "coffin life-buoy" reached the center of the vortex before Ishmael could be sucked into it, then shot up as the ship went under, propelled by the resulting jet of water. Ishmael clung to it and survived overnight. He was picked up by the *Rachel*, the following day. "In her retracing search after her missing children, [she] found another orphan" (1408).

Queequeg, the man of nature, in effect saved his friend by volunteering his coffin for use as a life-buoy, crafted and recrafted by the carpenter or mindless Christ. Ishmael was also saved by the captain of the *Rachel*, a man of familial moral sentiment and Biblical *agape*. Biblically-oriented readers will find in these and so many remarkable events prior to it the hand of Providence. Ishmael does not. Does Melville? Perhaps not, since after all his is the ruling intelligence behind the novel, and we have no way of knowing if he ascribed that gift to God.

*Chapter Fourteen*
# CONCLUDING THOUGHTS

The "Young America" movement aimed at speaking and acting for a new generation of Americans, as President John Kennedy would attempt to do, a century later, and as the 'New Left' would claim to do, only a few years after Kennedy. The passing of the torch of political authority from the older to the younger, or the wresting of that torch by the younger to the older, raises perennial questions: Will the fire light the way? Or will it burn the holder? Will it go out, causing the new bearer to stumble? Should it be snuffed out, and another torch lit? Should it be used to follow the same path, or should a new path be chosen?

In Melville's generation, Abraham Lincoln considered these questions in a lecture at the Young Men's Lyceum in Springfield, Illinois. "The Perpetuation of Our Political Institutions" was delivered and published thirteen years before the publication of *Moby-Dick*; its author was almost exactly the same age as Melville when he published his novel.[10] Like Melville, the young Lincoln has been said to have had his doubts about religion, although unlike Melville he could later claim to "have never spoken with intentional disrespect of religion in general."[11]

Lincoln invited his listeners to admire the American "system of political institutions," which "conduc[es] more essentially to the ends of civil and religion liberty than any of which the history of former times tells us." This "political edifice of liberty and equal rights" stands as "a legacy

10  Abraham Lincoln: "Address Before the Young Men's Lyceum of Springfield, Illinois." January 27, 1838. Ray P. Baler, ed. *The Collected Works of Abraham Lincoln*. New Brunswick: Rutgers University Press, 1953. I. 108–115.
11  Abraham Lincoln: "Handbill Replying to Charges of Infidelity." July 31, 1846. Basler I. 382.

bequeathed to us, by a *once* hardy, brave, patriotic, but *now* lamented and departed race of ancestors." Lincoln understood the duty of his generation of Americans to be the transmission of this legacy, "unprofaned by the foot of an invader," to the next generation. He found the prospect of foreign conquest remote. But the danger of self-ruin was real, as seen in recent instances of "mob law"—namely, the lynchings in Mississippi; or the extra-judicial execution by burning of a murderer in Missouri. When "the lawless in spirit" become "lawless in practice," law-abiding citizens will lose their trust in the government intended to secure their liberty and equal rights. If such citizens lose their attachment to the ruling institutions of a *republican* regime, then "the capability of a people to govern themselves" must come into question. This will give an opportunity to the supremely ambitious men who arise in every generation, men who "belong to the family of the lion, or the tribe of the eagle," men who "disdain the beaten path" of their ancestors to seek glory on any ground *other* than that taken by men who have gone before them. Only if citizens trust one another, and trust the government they have constituted and perpetuated, can such potential tyrants be defeated.

To reestablish or strengthen that trust, only reason can furnish new pillars for "the temple of liberty." Those materials can then "be molded into general intelligence, sound morality and, in particular, a reverence for the constitution and the laws"—for what Lincoln does not hesitate to call a "political religion." The old pillars of the temple were the Founders; the new pillars can only be men and women who emulate them, whose ambition finds its model not in an Alexander, a Caesar, or a Napoleon but in George Washington, that supremely self-governing statesman who has earned his status as first in war and first in peace among a people who intend to govern themselves, first of all by ruling their own passions.

When Melville published *Moby-Dick* in 1851, Americans ruled the middle section of North America from the Atlantic to the Pacific Ocean. If that rule could be consolidated by settlement, if disunion could be prevented, the United States would amount very nearly to a vast island, with oceans along its eastern and western borders, seas bordering it on much of the North and the South. Melville set out to caution Young America, to show his countrymen that the Pacific wasn't entirely pacific, that ocean waters surround all land on earth with chaos.[12] America's destiny may not be so manifest as Young America supposes. Is it as bright as they believe, given the real nature of 'the Pacific' Americans have arrived at? With Mexico and its ambitions to seize New Orleans defeated, if the remaining Amerindian nations and tribes are subdued, will Americans enjoy the prosperous peace they have sought in their wars? Lincoln worried that they might not, and those worries crested like a wave in the decade to follow. He saw the possibility of chaos on land, political chaos within the United States, in an intensifying regime conflict between the commercial-republican North and the slaveholding-oligarchic South, worsened by the moral and political conflict between political parties in the North.

For Lincoln saw in Young America—above all in his great Illinois rival, Senator Stephen Douglas—a threat to American self-government as dangerous as that posed by the plantation oligarchs of the South. Douglas, Lincoln averred, was "blowing out the moral lights around us" by refusing to navigate the popular sovereignty of the republican regime in America by the constellation of natural rights, the laws of Nature and of Nature's God, which had justified the Founders' assertion of that sovereignty against the sovereignty of the British tyrant.[13] To argue that the legal status of slaves in the newly-settled territories of the United States may be settle by popular votes in those territories—instead of by an appeal to the natural rights to equality and liberty enunciated by the Founders in the Declaration of Independence—overrode the rule of reason, valorizing the rule of passion. Law should secure natural rights; citizens should not suppose themselves entitled to vote the Laws of Nature and of Nature's God up or down.

Ahab represents nothing if not the family of the lion or the tribe of the (sea)-eagle. As such, he leaves himself morally vulnerable to having his captain's hat stolen by another eagle. Aboard the *Pequod*, no human being effectively opposes him, as Starbuck dithers, the crew alternately trembles and cheers, and Bulkington stays below deck. With *Moby-Dick*, however,

---

12  In this I depart from Charles Olson's account (op. cit., 116–119), which takes the Pacific Ocean to be genuinely pacific. Nothing that harbors Moby-Dick can be genuinely pacific. And then there are the typhoons.

13  Fifth Debate with Stephen A. Douglas. Galesburg, Illinois, October 4, 1858. Basler, op. cit., III. 234.

Melville opposes him, readying his readers to recognize and oppose him, too. To the mighty man, the might-makes-right man, Melville opposes the mighty book. A mighty book needs a mighty theme, Ishmael tells us. But mere might against might will not suffice. Don't merely 'enlarge' your mind, Ishmael tells us. "Subtilize it." Make it more discerning, more reasonable. The way to reasonableness isn't some 'system' of thought, philosophic or religious, but moderation of the soul's passions. Tempering the passions gives the mind a chance to think instead of only feeling. Ahab suggests that he who feels most intensely, whose feelings overwhelm other less coruscant souls, rightly rules them with a minimum of 'back-talk.' Melville writes to make citizens more thoughtful, more likely (among other things) to recognize an Ahab *as* a tyrant, as a person who may "have his humanities" but will not permit himself to be ruled by them, will not rule others by them, and thereby compromises the humanity of those he rules.

To subtilize the minds of Americans, Melville takes them to sea, where the chaotic dimension of nature must be faced. At sea one meets foreigners, men reared in regimes different from the American regime. Ishmael recalls "gams" or meetings with whaling ships from several countries. The Germans prove inexperienced, therefore lacking in practical judgment or prudence. They haven't ruled themselves long enough; the 'nation of philosophers' and of *Kultur* may mean well but it cannot yet do well, as it navigates often unstable seas. The French, too—landsmen, sometime upholders of the Rights of Man, accustomed to life under the centralized modern state— lack experience in self-government. The English do have such experience; what is more, their commercial way of life keeps them sane, but sometimes obscures from them the depths of the oceans upon which they sail so adeptly. As for the American ships the crew of the *Pequod* meet, they range from the self-indulgent to the compassionate. Which way will Americans take, in their regime?

They will need a modern state of some sort. With a decent regime, that state provides protection for women and children against human predators; it sends out expeditions, usually for commerce or, as with the America of Melville's time, expansion of its empire of liberty. Like all manifestations of the "weaver-god," it needs a framework for production. Given the chaotic dimension of the cosmos, it makes oligarchy difficult unless oligarchy embeds itself into the state's institutional framework in the form of bureaucracy—a move that wouldn't happen for nearly a century. Otherwise, as in the novel, the modern state's regime wavers between monarchy and democracy; under the well-designed framework of the American institutions, that had meant wavering between a strong Congress and a strong presidency. Democracy proves vulnerable to demagoguery and deception, whether religious or political. Founded as a tensile combination between 'Abraham' and 'Ishmael,' the American regime of 1851 saw threats from both Southern oligarchs and restive democrats, neither of which much heeded the moral limitations of natural right. While democrats lauded America's "Manifest Destiny" to rule the continent, Melville takes "destiny" as a danger, not an inevitable happy ending. A better Young America would understand nature or the chaos-cosmos of the weaver-god in a more careful way, soberly interweaving policy, including the policy of expansion, *within* the framework needed to support that 'god,' recognizing and avoiding demagogue-tyrants as they arise, encouraging commerce and industry without succumbing to venality. No aristocracy exists to guide Young America, but maybe Melville could. If, as one scholar puts it, Melville set himself the task of "reshap[ing] tragedy for a democratic (and American) audience,"[14] as a lesson in much-needed moderation, his hero's tragic flaw is dominant, his "humanities" recessive to the end.[15] Ahab rules his subjects by demagoguery, self-interest, and force, weapons lying around, as it were, in the commercial and democratic republican regime. Young America must learn to recognize such a man. It will fail to do so if immoderate, like the sailors, or if uncourageous—too timid, like Starbuck—or too rash and given to infect others with rashness, like Ahab. Ahab pits his personality against the impersonal weaver-god, but as John Alvis sees, "Personality is modernity's substitute for soul."[16] Melville doesn't think the

---

14 George Schulman: "Chasing the Whale: *Moby-Dick* as Political Theory." In Jason Frank, ed. *A Political Companion to Herman Melville*. Lexington: University Press of Kentucky, 2013, 71.

15 Olson makes much of Ahab's 'softening' under the effect of Pip's spirit (op. cit. 60–63). Ishmael makes it clear that he esteems the compassion Pip evokes—Ahab's one tear being worth more than all the water in the oceans—but he also observes how Ahab overcomes that compassion with an act of will, as if this were the last temptation of the anti-Christ.

16 John Alvis: "*Moby-Dick* and Melville's Quarrel with America." *Interpretation: A Journal of Political Philosophy.* Volume 23, Number 2, Winter 1996, 239.

soul immortal, in the Christian sense, but he does want Young America to remember the soul, and to take care of it. In this, he wants what Lincoln wanted.

The weaver-god hears no mortal voice as it intertwines life and death. The ancients called this cosmic interweaving force Fate, supposing they saw it behind all the personal gods of their pantheon. Trellised by a lifeless framework, like the God of the Bible the weaver-god respects no persons but (unlike God) only because it is impersonal, not because it is impartial or just. American Transcendentalists were wrong to suppose it benign. American Progressives would make the same mistake. Marx was wrong to expect it to issue in an inevitably happy outcome. Nietzsche would be wrong to love it, although his pessimism of strength echoes some of Melville's thoughts, even as it amplifies them too much. Transcendentalists has chosen the wrong symbolism to depict it; Melville deploys symbolism, too—indeed, having some wicked fun with the Transcendentalists' symbols in so doing—but makes it compatible with his stern realism. Fate leaves room for chance or fortune, for randomness, also for human custom; despite these severe limitations, human beings can still ply the shuttle, exercise a modest freedom for good or evil. In politics, therefore, revolution or regime change and modest reform remain possible, although they require virtue and good fortune for success. The philosophic founders of modern science supposed that human beings can use their freedom to conquer nature and fortune; Melville thinks not. The ocean is too big. If he could see the technologies of later centuries, he would continue to say the ocean is too big to be mastered, pointing to the near-limitless cosmos beyond earth, with its imploding and exploding stars, its snake-spiraling nebulae (with their microcosmic counterparts, snake-stranding DNA), and its overall entropic careening, as an even more decisive refutation of human pretension. If the chaos-cosmos could speak, it, too, could ask the devastating rhetorical question, "Where were you when I created the heavens and the earth?" Melville provides nature a sort of voice, derived from his experience of the ocean.

This is why his narrator commands us to call him Ishmael. His father sired him when he was still "Abram." Only after Abram accepts the covenant with God does he become Abraham—the awe-inspired 'H' of God now stamped on his name, defining him and his son, Isaac. Born of

Sarah, a freewoman, Isaac will freely serve God. Sired with a slave-woman, Hagar, Ishmael "was born after the flesh," the Apostle Paul tells the Galatians (Galatians 4:23). Melville's Ishmael is also a child of the flesh, not of the covenant with God; he points us to a realistic understanding of nature, locating right in it while locating evil there, too. If Young America keeps the covenant with God, so prominent in the Great Awakening that flourished during Melville's childhood, Melville would have it a Christianity skeptical of churchiness and mindful of the dangers of self-righteousness. He reminds American Christians that Jesus was a Man of Sorrows. If Young America instead adheres to the flesh, to nature, Melville would rank Rousseau also among the men of sorrows and, while reserving a place for a 'Rousseauian' inner Tahiti, a good and peaceful core in human and non-human nature, he would never let it forget that much of nature will break and kill you without caring.

Rightly so humbled, human beings may still have self-knowledge and a measure of self-protection if they exercise genuine moderation, not Starbuck's false moderation. "In all seasons retain a temperature of thine own." If you don't, you won't understand the underlying foundation of the chaos-cosmos, as in your thinking you will finally face the blank wall that tormented Ahab. It need not torment you, as it does him, leading him to ruin. You may never understand how or why human freedom can arise in the chaos-cosmos of fate. The blank wall Ahab finds at the end of his speculative thought defeats doctrines and systems religious or philosophic, but a mind alert to practical matters—how a ship works, how a political regime and a modern state work, and how such things might be made to work better—will find its inner Tahiti. Two deformations of Melville's thought might come from this: pragmatism, which in American thought would put itself in the service of nature-conquest; and Epicureanism, an apolitical withdrawal from one's country. Regarding the latter, Melville's Ishmael may be an outsider, but he spins his yarn anyway, and Melville never set out for the territories to live as a hermit. He continued to intervene in American politics in his subsequent writings.

What will guide practical reason? The chaos-cosmos, nature, may not lend itself to a *doctrine* of natural right, as the American founding generation maintained, but nature isn't evil if treated with moderation and faced with courage. At its generative, original, 'sperm' level of being nature is pure, cleansing, offering human beings a natural baptism if not a foundation a for systematic natural religion. Nature affords a place for friendship and fraternity, so long as you don't stare too long in the face of its fire, and so long as you accept its carpenter-Christ as impersonal, the Christ of the Bible as human, as a *man* of sorrows. This is as far as flesh-born Ishmael will go, or can go, if he remains a natural man.

Leviathan, the king of the proud, combines the bulk of the land with the movement of water; Leviathan's spout mixes water with air. The 'H' of the word 'whale' denotes beholding, beholding the *haishim*, the fiery 'souls' of atoms postulated by Lucretius. Earth, water, air, fire: nature unites and balances opposites, as can its political equivalent, the modern state, in Mr. Madison's version. Nature is cannibalistic, self-devouring, a matter of life and death. The right way to understand it is with a pantheism of pessimism, a pessimism of strength. Expect little from it; do not be so foolish as to love it; reserve the agapic love Christianity teaches and the friendship-love of citizens for those fellow-humans who need and deserve it. The (perhaps) self-generating chaos-cosmos will kill you, but in so doing self-regenerates, self-repairs. Cold comfort that is, but warmer comforts, material and soulful, remain to you in the meantime.

Ahab understands some of this, but not nearly enough. To the modern tyrant's soul, 'Being' is *alogos*, a thing rightly worshiped only in defiance. In the plays of Shakespeare Melville so admired, he would rank with Richard III, not Lear or Prospero. Unlike Richard, however, he burns with ambitions beyond absolute rule; unlike subsequent tyrants, he has no 'ideological' ambitions. Ahab's ambitions are spiritual-metaphysical. He rejects all that is 'above' him, navigating only by the 'horizontal,' what is around him. In this he partakes of democracy even as he tyrannizes, a practice Tocqueville would have expected having studied Napoleon. Ahab contradicts himself, repeatedly, having taken the fluid sea as his solid rock. No human being can stand on that rock, much less walk on water. Ahab would have needed to do one or the other, but he doesn't want to be a man and he cannot be a god. After the fact, Ishmael rightly interprets the typhoon lightning strikes in Biblical terms—specifically, in terms of the Book of Daniel. Ishmael finds in Biblical prophecy cogent explanations of what *has* happened; he never 'prophesies' or predicts, claiming no access to the thoughts of a personal god. Charles Olson rightly understands Ishmael as the chorus for a tragedy in the form of a novel, not as a would-be prophet.[17]

Ahab's days were numbered; he had been weighed, found wanting; his state would split, sundered by the nature it sought to defeat. His regime, too, must split because its sole, a-logical ruler is 'split' among his many self-contradictions, even as his ship will be 'staved' by Moby-Dick. Fire-worshipers crave freedom, but in gazing at the fire too long they become only greater slaves to fate, thinking not wisely but too wishfully according to the false prophets they follow. Ahab would 'save' himself and even triumph by pil[ing] on the whale's white hump the sum of all the general rage and hate felt by his whole race from Adam down." Yet there is no reason to suppose that killing the Whale would cure Ahab's soul; the chaos-cosmos will remain, whatever becomes of its symbol. (Manipulators of images and words, take notice). Ishmael, who shares Ahab's estimate of the whiteness of the Whale—"the palsied universe […] lies before us a leper"—wisely avoids Ahab's rage at it. Caught up in the general enthusiasm of the crew at crucial moments, and therefore no fit ruler, his soul reclaims its balance for the most part and in the end. Unlike his tyrant-captain, he does not weep over "The Symphony" of the elements, having so much less to regret. He sees that even at its most pacific, the seabirds who skim the ocean's surface are as white as the whale. Whiteness dominates the ocean tyrannically only when something or someone roils it. Ishmael seldom does.

If our souls are like orphans of unwed mothers, their fathers unknown, then philosophy must take a Socratic turn. That is, if orthodoxy, tradition, can mislead and if credulity can be foolish, so can incredulity. We don't know enough for either. Ishmael scoffs at religious doctrines, but equally at the pretenses of modern science. Socratic inquiry—rational examination of the orthodoxies and observations of the many human 'types' one meets in the marketplace—is what politics and political philosophers can do. As for religious men, Solomon is the one Ishmael esteems, for his practical wisdom in speech and action. And if Socrates and Solomon are the Catskill eagles among men, the average citizen may need to think as the old Manx-

---

17  Olson, op. cit., 58. Ishmael is, however, a *one-man* chorus, an 'isolato' chorus; he does not represent the opinions of any political community.

man does, with common sense.[18] Morally, his exemplar may well be the natural man, Queequeg—natural even to the point of cannibalism, in emulation of all nature—but also courageous, resourceful, adaptable to all regimes, a loyal friend, a wanderer and wonderer, like Ishmael. Ishmael doesn't follow his friend into cannibalism of the literal kind, but he does argue that in a pantheistic universe we are all cannibals by necessity, himself included—all part of self-devouring, self-regenerating nature in one way or another. The 'marriage' or friendship of Queequeg and Ishmael serves as the equivalent of real marriage in Aristotle: the possible foundation of political life, pairing a potential philosopher or (at least) an 'intellectual' with a man of courage, of action—the alliance of reason and spiritedness, philosophy and kingliness commended by Socrates in Plato's *Republic*.

Wanderers won't make citizens, however, so the Queequeg-Ishmael friendship is highly unlikely to result in a real political community. Even on Ahab's ship of state, Queequeg's ineluctable foreignness and Ishmael's 'isolato' predisposition (wavering between his habit of holding back to observe and learn and his occasional bouts of enthusiastic communal fellow feeling) preclude any effective political action. Wanderers and waverers won't make citizens. Neither will philosophers, entirely. They will always hold fast in their inner core, observing and reasoning about their observations. Like citizens, philosophers will form friendships. They can become political philosophers, not isolatoes. If friendly, un-philosophic citizens also learn to recognize the kinds of men who endanger friendship, the tyrants, they can govern themselves. They need to see the virtues of Queequeg and Ishmael, as described by a political-philosophic poet, to strengthen themselves, and to smarten themselves up, for such civic friendship. Most will never become a Queequeg or an Ishmael, but most can learn things from them.

A decade after Melville published *Moby-Dick*, he and his fellow-Americans saw their own national tragedy, in which Ishmaels and Queequegs,

18   Olson sees the Catskill eagle in Ishmael (op. cit. 15) but misses the common sense in the Manxman. He must, because he takes the American *people* to be represented by Ishmael, whereas Melville knows that an Ishmael must always be the exception, not the rule. In this, Olson failed to learn from Nietzsche, his favorite among philosophers.

Ahabs, Starbucks, Stubbses, and Flasks, along with many of the other character types in the novel, and some not there, came forward to enact a regime conflict 'for real.' Melville acted as the chorus in that tragedy, writing his poems collected as *Battle-Pieces* as the events of the war coursed from beginning to end. Young America matured, then, learning from experience some of the things they might have learned at lesser cost, had they paid attention to Melville in the first place.

# *MOBY-DICK* IN PRACTICE: MELVILLE'S *BATTLE-PIECES*[19]

Melville calls the American Civil War a "historic tragedy" which he hopes has "not been enacted without instructing our whole beloved country through terror and pity" ("Supplement," 232). *Moby-Dick* is a tragedy in the form of a novel, centering on the fundamentals of human being in nature; through terror and pity, Melville instructs his readers on self-government and tyranny. In his book on the Civil War, Melville shows how the tragic knowledge imparted by *Moby-Dick* may guide American citizens in practice. In the language of some of the old philosophers, he shows how theoretical wisdom can inform practical wisdom, how the principles distilled from the novel may guide citizens' deliberation in and after a political crisis. In this he takes his guidance from Shakespeare, as he had done when writing his novel:

No utter surprise can come to him
Who reaches Shakespeare's core;
That which we seek and shun is there—
Man's final lore.

("The Coming Storm: A Picture by S. R. Gifford and Owned by F. B. Included in the N. A. Exhibition: April, 1865")

---

19  References to the text are drawn from the facsimile edition of *Battle-Pieces and Aspects of the War* published by Da Capo Press, New York, 1995. Readers may also wish to consult the excellent critical edition edited by Richard H. Cox and Paul M. Dowling, published by Prometheus Books, Amherst, 2001.

There is in man, and therefore in the Civil War and its aftermath, so much to attract and to repel those who look into him, that we need a guide. For Melville, that guide is Shakespeare, poet of tragic kings and civil wars, above all others; he would be Shakespeare for his own people.

The literary critic Edmund Wilson complained that *Battle-Pieces* was written by a man who never saw a single battle in the war.[20] That is no ground for complaint. This is a book by a civilian, for civilians, speaking as one citizen to another, conveying the civilian experience of modern war and concluding with considerations centering on the need for civilians to restore civil peace on new terms. Having won the war, Northerners, how shall you win the peace? How shall you restore the Union you fought for? And what will the character of that Union be? Civil wars are revolutionary wars, wars over regimes. Will the democratic and commercial republic conceived in 1776 survive? Or will it fall apart, defeated politically after the war not by a regime ruled by slaveholding oligarchs, but by the factions that have survived the war? "We have sung of the soldiers and sailors, but who shall hymn the politicians? ("Supplement," 259) Melville writes a poetic 'reconstruction' of the war in service of a moderate political 'reconstruction.'

America's historical tragedy differed from Melville's prose tragedy from the outset. The Ahab-figure, tyrannic-souled John Brown, died before the war began, although he may be said to have portended the war in his violent life and death.[21] And, as Stanton Garner argues, the narrator of *Battle-Pieces* isn't a fictional Ishmael but Melville himself, the chorus of the tragedy.[22]

---

20  Edmund Wilson: *Patriotic Gore: Studies in the Literature of the American Civil War.* New York: Oxford University Press, 1962, p. 479.

21  Paul Dowling astutely calls attention to Brown's Southern counterpart, Edmund Ruffin, who (Melville remarks) fired the first shot of the Civil War at Fort Sumter and committed suicide in Richmond at the end of the war. Both North and South had their 'Ahab.' But only one had Lincoln, and he would be murdered by a Southern Fedallah. See Dowling, "Melville's Quarrel with Poetry," Cox and Dowling, eds., op. cit., 345–356.

22  Stanton Garner: *The Civil War World of Herman Melville.* Lawrence: University Press of Kansas, 1993. Garner's meticulous account of Melville's life during the war includes careful exegeses of the poems; Cox and Dowling examine several of the most important poems with even greater attention to detail, of-

The American nation takes the place of the tragic hero or anti-hero; the author speaks directly, when he is not presenting the many American voices heard in his 72 poems. Here, the protagonist is 'the many,' the chorus only 'one.' The democracy does not exclaim, advise, weep for the monarch; the author, the ruler of the book, exclaims, advises, weeps for the democracy where "The People spread like weedy grass," their impassioned factiousness having caused "the Founders' dream" to "flee," despite their founding attempt to temper faction with republican institutions ("The Conflict of Conviction [1860–61]," 15–17).

To this factionalism, Melville opposes thought, not additional 'lyric' passion. Romantic Wordsworth had called "emotion recollected in tranquility" the origin of poetry; Melville recollects his and his nation's emotions in anxiety, in caution. "I muse upon my country's ills," he announces, "on the world's fairest hope"—the American republic, dedicated to the proposition that all men are created equal—"linked with man's foulest crime" ("Misgivings [1861], 13). Most commentators identify this crime as slavery, the terrifying and pitiable flaw in the regime dedicated to equality of unalienable natural rights; Garner suspects that Melville means fratricide, not America's but man's foulest crime, the crime of Cain against Abel, now seen in the war of brother against brother. Since, as Lincoln argued, American slavery—cousin of fratricide, a crime committed (in its American version) by members of one race of men against members of another race—and since that slavery infuriated the American Ahab, John Brown, who brought America near to the catastrophe of the *Pequod*, one need not choose. The two crimes

---

fering a brilliant analysis of the way Melville structured his book. Although they all rightly describe Melville as a poet of moderation, they differ regarding what that moderation consisted of, interpreting Melville's politics differently as a consequence. Garner argues for Melville as a Northern Democrat, an admirer of General George McClellan; Cox and Dowling regard Melville as a Lincoln man. I concur with the latter judgment, for the most part, but find it significant that a serious case can be made for both positions. Melville's prudence and moderation, remarked by all three scholars, lend themselves to such politic ambiguity. Melville wrote a book that might bind up at least some of the nation's wounds, precisely by inviting many citizens of various convictions to think while reading, 'Those are my thoughts'—often the best strategy for carefully modifying such thoughts.

are the same kind of crime, attempts to make natural right a "loose-fish." As in *Moby-Dick*, so in America: "Nature's dark side is heeded now" (Ibid. 13); "Satan's old age is strong and hale" ("The Conflict of Convictions," 14).

The Founders' dream, the bright dream of a natural-rights republic, established in reality but flawed like all real things, flawed by the dark line of slave-mastery, impassioned and impassionating, fired the nightmare of John C. Calhoun's republic, founded on that mastery. Nature's God will settle the matter:

The light and the dark:
Yea and Nay—
Each hath its say;
But God He keeps the middle way.
("The Conflict of Convictions," 18)

Musing on the Civil War, Melville finds no Hegelian synthesis of thesis and antithesis, of yea and nay, instead recurring to the Aristotelian principle of 'the mean,' of moderation—as Cox and Dowling emphasize.[23] Melville was right: In practical terms, Hegelian logic has produced political extremes, the fanatic 'totalitarianism' of latter-day John Browns. But "Wisdom is vain, and prophecy." (Ibid. 18) As in *Moby-Dick*, grand systems of reason or of revelation animate the tragic victims and fools of nature.

Youth must its ignorant impulse lend—
Age finds place in the rear.
All wars are boyish, and are fought by boys,
The champions and enthusiasts of the state:
Turbid ardors and vain joys
Not barrenly abate—
Stimulants to the power mature,
Preparatives of fate.
("The March into Virginia: Ending in the First Manassas, July 1861," 22)

---

23   Richard H. Cox and Paul M. Dowling: "Herman Melville's Civil War: Lincolnian Prudence in Poetry." *The Political Science Reviewer*. Volume XXIX, 2000, 192–295.

What fate is that? "It is enough," Melville answers, "for all practical purposes, if the South have been taught by the terrors of civil war to feel that
Secession, like Slavery, is against Destiny; that both now lie buried in one
grave; that her fate is linked with ours; and that together we comprise the
Nation" ("Supplement," 260). The pre-war regimes of the Southern states
put the people "in subserviency to the slave-interest," which "cajoled" the
people "into revolution against the United States by "plausibly urg[ing] that
certain inestimable rights guaranteed by the Constitution were directly
menaced" by the election of Abraham Lincoln. Plausibly but wrongly: "The
most sensitive love of liberty was entrapped into the support of a war whose
implied end was erecting in our advanced century an Anglo-American Empire based on the systematic degradation of man" ("Supplement," 261).
"Fate" here isn't Hegel's Absolute Spirit or Marxian historical dialectic; it is
nature's shutting-down of self-contradiction, its punishment of the 'fatal
flaw' within the tragic hero, whether an individual or a people. "Nature is
nobody's ally"; it wounds or kills any person or nation violating it, impar-
tially ("Dupont: Round Fight, November, 1861," 32).

Melville reconstructs the war by following nature-fate's successive 'revelation,' responses to impassioned, partisan illusions of both sides.
"Prophetic, sad" General Nathaniel Lyon became the first Union general
to be killed in the war, sorrowfully going into a battle in which he was out-
numbered two-to-one by the Confederate forces near Springfield, Missouri
("Lyon: Battle of Springfield, Missouri, August, 1861," 23). His men inflicted heavy losses on the Rebels that day, saving Missouri from Confederate control. By contrast, General George McClellan lost the Battle of
Bull's Bluff, near Loudon, Virginia, in October 1861; this and other early
battles saw Northern youth, in whom "Life throbbed so strong," feeling
"immortal, like the gods sublime," crushed by their Southern counterparts,
defeats triggering a Congressional inquiry into why the Union was losing
the war ("Bull's Bluff: A Reverie, October, 1861," 28).

At sea and on the rivers, ship-battles revealed the modern way of war,
the way not of the sailing ships Melville depicted in *Moby-Dick* but of the
"utilitarian," unheroic, decidedly un-aesthetic ironclad *Monitor*, bring "victory without the gaud of glory" with "sheer mechanic power." The *Monitor*
and its replicas place war "where War belongs—among the trades and ar-
tisans," beyond "passion": "The anvil-din / Resounds this message from the

Fates," namely, that "warriors are now but operatives," war itself now "less grand than Peace" ("A Utilitarian View of the Monitor's Fight," 61–62). That may be a very good, sobering thing, but it will require a calmer sort of courage than hitherto required of sailors—as seen on land, also, in the Battle of Antietam, still the bloodiest day in American history.

There, McClellan's forces repelled Lee's at Sharpsburg, Maryland, stopping the Confederate advance into the state, but McClellan over-cautiously allowed the attackers to escape. Melville's nod to the poem is masterpiece of ambiguous praise ("whatever just military criticism, favorable or otherwise, has at any time been made upon General McClellan's campaigns, will stand") and the poem itself, spoken by a former soldier under his command, itself praises a bit faintly: "Unprosperously heroical!" "[Y]ou did your best, as in you lay, McClellan" ("The Victor at Antietam, 1862," 69–71). On the Confederate side, a far greater general in a far worse cause, Stonewall Jackson rates compassion but not praise from a Unionist ("Justly his fame we outlaw; so / We drop a tear on the bold Virginian's bier / Because no wreath we owe"), fuller-throated tribute from a fellow Virginian (for "his Roman heart" and "great soul") ("Stonewall Jackson: Mortally Wounded at Chancellorsville May, 1863," 86–87). In honoring Pickett's charge during the Battle of Gettysburg, Melville has prepared his readers for a moral foundation for Reconstruction: On Cemetery Hill, "*every* bone shall rest in honor" ("Gettysburg: The Check, July, 1863," 85).

The book's polyphony serves a political purpose. Without descending into moral relativism—at Gettysburg, "Pride was rebelled by sterner pride, / And Right is a stronghold, yet"—he presents the voices of citizens who must bind themselves together now, after the war. (ibid. 84–85) He wants Americans to listen to one another, and to respect one another, again, as they had not done in the decade between the publication of *Moby-Dick* and the assault on Fort Sumter. In the face of the "Atheist roar of riot" heard in New York from the violent draft resisters as they torched the city, in apparent confirmation of "Calvin's creed" of original sin and of the "cynic tyrannies of honest kings," the Draconian imposition of peace redeemed "the Town," threatened by "The grimy slur on the Republic's faith implied, / Which holds that Man is naturally good" ("The House-Top: A Night Piece, July, 1863," 86–87). New York's Publius (it might be noted) thought neither Calvin nor Rousseau right, simply, nor did the author of *Moby-*

*Dick.*[24] As the narrator of the poem "Chattanooga" reminds General Grant, "You must know your men" ("Chattanooga, November, 1863," 90). Melville wants Americans to know themselves better. Only then can they reunite on a just and reasonable foundation.

The main section of *Battle-Pieces* contains fifty-three poems, the twenty-seventh or central being "The Armies of the Wilderness (1863–65)." The Civil War itself was a wilderness in which the nation lost its way. In that campaign, in Virginia, Grant and Lee played cat and mouse, and for a long time it was not known who was to prove the cat, who the mouse. Animated by "feudal fidelity" (ibid. 97) to the aristocrat-oligarchs commanding him, a Confederate captive refuses to betray his comrades by giving information to his captors. When they ask him where General Lee is, he ripostes, "In the hearts and bayonets of all yon men!" (ibid. 95) For his part, General Grant's heart is "calm as the Cyclone's core" (ibid. 101)— that new form of courage, seen in the new kind of sailors, too. Melville's narrator compares the forest-fire smoke raised by rival armies at Spotsylvania to the Pillar of Fire which led the Israelites through their wilderness; American troops on both sides find not an answer but a riddle, "A riddle of death, of which the slain / Sole survivors are" (ibid. 103). In a poem honoring a corps commander in the battle (Union man or Rebel?), he recalls the heroes of Agincourt "who shared great Harry's mind" because nature is nature, regardless of time or place, and nature, though "oft remiss," does produced eagles ("A Photograph of a Corps Commander," 105). Melville points his readers to nature, not to God:

Nothing can lift the heart of man
Like manhood in a fellow-man.
The thought of heaven's great King afar
But humbles us—too weak to scan;

24   Garner, op. cit., suggests that the narrator of the poem on the riots is a self-conceived Anglo-American 'aristocrat,' sniffing at the unruly (and largely Irish) *polloi*. This comports with his claim that Melville is a Northern Democrat who prefers McClellan to Lincoln, and therefore sympathizes with the rioters. My own view is that Melville deliberately eludes such straightforward, partisan categories.

But manly greatness men can span,
And feel the bonds that draw.
(ibid. 106)

Those natural bonds are the ones which can help to bind the Union together, Melville hopes, even as Jefferson had hoped they would, as he wrote
the Declaration of Independence.

Its spiritual heart in "the proud City" of Charleston, South Carolina,
the Confederate regime was founded on the Calhounian principle that all
men are not created equal, and so cannot share a natural bond secured by
civil institutions, unless that bond derives from a race within the human
species, not from humanity itself. Charleston falls victim to the "coal-black"
Swamp Angel, the Parrott gun used to bombard it, dooming the city "by
far decree"; the symbol of black former slaves who smashed St. Michael's
church, the church of "aristocratic" Charlestonians, the church named for
"the white man's seraph," who fled the city whose rulers worshiped at his
shrine. In the Bible, Archangel Michael, leader of the Army of God, the
heavenly host, escorts the faithful to Heaven at their hour of death, but the
aristocrat-angels of Charleston, eminences of 'slaveocracy,' found no refuge
from the Union's 'angel' of death. Mindful of the need for national recon-
ciliation, Melville appeals to the piety of his Northern readers, not their
triumphalism or their passion for revenge:

Who weeps for the woeful City
Let him weep for our guilty kind;
Who joys at her wild despairing—
Christ, the forgiver, convert his mind.
(ibid. 109)

It was, after all, Christian piety that drove the movement to abolish slavery,
not simply esteem for natural right. After accomplishing that good, Christians must now find a way to restore civil peace. And as readers know from
*Moby-Dick*, Christian sentiment may not suffice. Melville's acknowledg-
ment that our "kind," our nature, is "guilty" shows that republican faith in
the goodness of human beings must be tempered by Publius' recognition
of their darker side, a recognition that Publius shares with Calvin and the

Bible itself—a recognition necessary precisely for republican regimes if they are to secure the natural rights of their citizens.

Melville shows how difficult Reconstruction will be, invoking fresh memories of the military prison camps maintained by both regimes ("In the Prison Pen," "The College Colonel," and "On the Natural Monument in a field of Georgia"), the deaths of heroes like Jackson and, on the Union side, Major General James B. McPherson. Above all of these, however, looms the brilliant but devastating march to the sea led by General William Tecumseh Sherman, whom Southerners "will long remember" in hatred ("The March to the Sea, December, 1864," 132). Melville recognizes the military necessity of the march, the jubilation of the freed slaves who joined the march, and the political necessity of breaking the slaveholder oligarchy. He greets the later fall of Richmond with forthright approbation: "Right through might is Law" now ("The Fall of Richmond, 1866," 136). But he knows that for many Southerners, President Lincoln, "by nature the most kindly of men, authorized Sherman's march, thereby fortifying his reputation among them as "the personification of tyrannic power"; even worse, "each Union soldier was called a Lincolnite" ("The Frenzy in the WAK: Sherman's March through the Carolinas, February 1865," 205 n. N). For reunion to take hold, Southerners and Union soldiers must let go of their mutual hostility.

Consistent with the teaching of *Moby-Dick*, Melville hardly assumes that this benign outcome will occur. His "Canticle" respecting "the national exaltation of enthusiasm at the close of the war" begins by celebrating the American nation, which "moves in power, not pride," with a "devotion" as deep "as Humanity is wide." He goes so far as to offer "Hosanna to the Lord of hosts," that Lord being "human kind"; this is no sequel to the Battle Hymn of the Republic. The rainbow covenant "rekindled" in its brightness here is the national covenant, the Constitution, the covenant among citizens. But even as "repose is in the air," "the foamy deep; unsounded" lies beneath it, and in the deep "the Giant of the Pool / Heaves his forehead white as wool— / Toward the Iris ever climbing / From the Cataracts that call—." The White Whale, the Ancient of Days, remains below, even as Humanity grows "toward the fullness of her fate" ("A Canticle: Significant of the National Exaltation of Enthusiasm at the Close of the War," 139–140).

The poem immediately following responds to the murder of Abraham Lincoln on Good Friday 1865. In a final act of treachery ("they killed him from behind"), the rebels "killed him in his prime / Of clemency and calm— / When with yearning he was filled / To redeem the evil-willed, / And, though conqueror, be kind." The People, ever prone to passion, now will "bare the iron hand," once they are done mourning. At the time, Melville explains in a note, Vice President Andrew Johnson was expected to be harsher with the South than Lincoln would have been, although "happily for the country," those expectations have not been fulfilled. The Congressional Republicans would be a different matter, the real "Avenger" or the "Forgiver," the agent of popular rage ("The Martyr: Indicative of the passion of the people on the 15ᵗʰ of April, 1865," 141–142). Anticipating this, Melville writes "a plea against the vindictive cry raised by civilian shortly after the surrender at Appomattox." Melville asks his readers to understand "rebel color-bearers" at Shiloh as "martyrs for the Wrong" but martyrs still: "Perish their Cause! But mark the men." And "think how Grant met Lee"—with dignified forbearance, even as he required unconditional surrender ("Rebel Color-bearers at Shiloh," 144–145). The rainbow of the renewed covenant will last only if Nature *dis*bands another light, the Aurora-Borealis, the "Northern lights," symbolizing the Union armies, whose "steely play" still flashes at the end of the dark night of civil war ("Aurora-Borealis: Commemorative of the Dissolution of the Armies at the Peace, May, 1865," 148–149). God (nature, fate) commanded both the war and its end, but it will be up to Americans, and especially citizens of the victorious North, to renew the work of self-government again, at dawn.

Melville continues to identify obstacles to this work. A Rebel soldier, released from prison, finds himself in New York City—or as he regards it, the "Nineveh of the North"—awaiting his return home. "But home he shall never see, / Even if he should stand upon the spot," as it is "gone," destroyed by the Union troops. And although the rebellion has failed, rebelliousness remains; Melville can only hope that guns buried near sacked Southern cities, intended for use upon return, will remain in their graves ("The Released Rebel Prisoner, June, 1865," 15–17). And the longest poem of the collection, "The Scout Toward Aldie," which Melville places apart from the main body of his book, hints at a more sinister possible issuance.

In spring 1864 Melville and his brother Allan visited their cousin Henry Gansevoort at his army camp in the Shenandoah Valley of Virginia. Melville went on a three-day sortie or "scout" in search of the Confederate lawyer-turned-guerrilla leader John Mosby. With a verse recalling *Moby-Dick*—"As glides in seas the shark, / Rides Mosby through green dark"—Melville begins to covey the pervasive menace of modern guerrilla warfare ("The Scout toward Aldie," 187). Mosby's Rangers tactics consisted of striking, retreating, then blending back into their farms and villages, seldom betrayed by their families and neighbors. The green dark of forests and swamps would become much too familiar to American soldiers fighting in the wars of the next century. "The Grey Ghost" would survive the war; during it, "All spake of him, but few had seen / Except the maimed ones or the low; / Yet rumor made him every thing— / A farmer—woodman—refugee— / The man who crossed the field but now; / A spell about his life did cling" (ibid. 187–188). Although Mosby himself never continued his shark-attacks after the surrender, his spirit haunted the aftermath, as the great Confederate cavalry commander (and lawless antebellum slave-trader) Nathan Bedford Forrest turned the guerrilla warriors of the newly-formed Ku Klux Klan on civilian freedmen, terrorizing many into submission and frustrating the policy of Reconstruction or thoroughgoing regime change. In a poetic meditation on a painted portrait of a former slave by E. Vedder, Melville predicts that only "her children's children" will know "the good withheld from her" ("'Formerly a Slave: An Idealized Portrait by E. Vedder," 154). The bitterness of ex-Confederates, the likelihood of continued military resistance in the form of what later generations would call asymmetrical warfare, and the scars of slavery on the freemen all augur poorly for reunion.

As in *Moby-Dick*, so in America:
So, then, Solidity's a crust—
The core of fire below;
All may go well for many a year,
But who can think without a fear
Of horrors that happen so?
("The Apparition [A Retrospect]," 155)

And even if the Northern men reach out hands of friendship in magnanimity, what might have been the only answering hands in the South may now be dead.

Melville concludes the main section of his book with his own "Gettysburg Address." In his poem "America" he likens the American flag to Berenice's hair—the constellation named for the ancient Egyptian queen who sacrificed her hair as a votive offering, hoping that her husband, Ptolemy III, would return safely from his campaign in Syria. The American flag flew over a land that "reposed in peace," a peace rent by the lightning of war ("America," 161). Berenice/America fell asleep during that war, dreaming not in hope, as the Founders had, but in terror:

A silent vision unavowed,
Revealing earth's foundation bare,
And Gorgon in her hidden place.
It was a thing of fear to see
So foul a dream upon so fair a face,
And the dreamer lying in that starry shroud.
("America," 161)

This means that America, all Americans, have seen what Pip saw, afloat and abandoned at sea. Unlike Pip, however, the people have restored their reason, put aside the passions that nearly destroyed their country. Having seen the green dark where the shark-profile of the Grey Ghost glides after its prey, having seen the undulating snake-hair of Gorgon, Americans now know the darker dimensions of nature. Awakening, America recovers, gazing to heaven with "a clear calm look" in pain, "but such as purifies the stain," and "with hope grown wise." With "law on her brow and empire in her eyes"—the empire of liberty, won in the first half of the century only to be nearly lost in the war—America now stands high, "on the crag," like an eagle (ibid. 162). This recalls the imagery of an earlier, seemingly anomalous poem, "The Eagle of the Blue." In it, Melville recalled a live eagle that some of the Union regiments brought to battle with them, whose "eager calm of gaze intent" foresaw victory. "The very rebel looks and thrills" at the eagle, which survived the war. "Well may we think his years are charmed" ("The Eagle of the Blue," 122–123). Charmed, because the eagle's country worked with nature, not against it, as tyrant Ahab did not and as

Ishmael learned to do, both in quest of a sight of the Whale, but only one seeing how to live in a cosmos with it.[25]

Malice toward none, charity toward all: In Melville's account, Robert E. Lee exhibited the one, hoped for the other. Unlike Mosby, the lawyer who operated outside the law, Lee was a warrior who wished to reestablish law. In testifying before Congress in April 1866, "no word he breathe[d] in vain lament"; he accepted the verdict of nature or fate and "acquiesce[d] in asserted laws." "Who looks at Lee must think of Washington," that other great secessionist general, if in a far better 'Cause.' "Push not your triumph," he tells the Congressmen; "do not urge submissiveness beyond the verge." "To elect magnanimity is wise," and the "fruit" of victory, considered with greatness of soul, is "re-established law." This is so, because if it is to be just,

---

25   The last two lines of "The Eagle of the Blue" echo rhythmically the last lines of Tennyson's poem, "The Lady of Shalott." On her island in a river near Camelot, the Lady is cursed; to occupy her time she weaves her "charmed web," but she may not look at reality directly, viewing passersby on the road to Camelot through a mirror and depicting them in her tapestries. She is a weaver, as Ishmael and Queequeg were, and as nature is. "Sick of shadows," when she sees "bold Sir Lancelot," his armor shining, singing, she turns away from the mirror and the loom to see him directly. The mirror cracks, "The curse is come upon me"; she sets out for Camelot on a boat, "chanting her deathsong." When her boat arrives, she is dead. Lancelot sees her, saying, "God in his mercy grant her grace, / The Lady of Shalott." Melville's novel, Melville's poems, are the tapestries which picture reality for those not yet ready to see it straight on.

As for the Union regimental eagle, it resembles the eagle in another Tennyson poem; like that eagle, "his claw has known the crag." Far from an artist who cannot face reality without bringing down destruction to himself, the Eagle of the Blue "exulteth in the war" with a "pride of quenchless strength." "Though scarred in many a furious fray, / No deadly hurt he knew; / Well may we think his years are charmed— / The Eagle of the Blue." Unlike Tennyson's Lady, the eagle faces reality and survives; far from cursed, it is charmed. As a poet Melville insists on looking at reality requires that his readers look at it, at least indirectly, and celebrates the symbol of the Union whose soldiers did look directly at reality. For Melville, the true weaver is nature/fate, and human beings and their regimes survive only if they know how to live within its tapestry as it binds them, with moderation, good judgment, and sympathy for their fellows, all of whom live and die within those conditions.

law requires recognition of nature, which in human beings finds its ground in love of its own in home and family, which most Southerners thought of themselves as defending in the war. "Was this the unforgivable sin? / These noble spirits are yet yours to win." Do not act like Europeans, with their monarchic regimes; "avoid the tyranny you reprobate" ("Lee in the Capital, April, 1866," 234–237).

Which is it, though? Given that "Secession, like Slavery," is *contra natura*, "against Destiny" ("Supplement," 200), against the lessons *Moby-Dick* teaches with words and the Civil War taught in harsh deeds, what then? The dead hand of the South grasped in vain by the magnanimous North? The guerrilla-terrorism of Forrest? Or reunion with noble Southerners who will reciprocate if only Northerners understand them? Melville hopes it is the latter, offering "A Meditation attributed to a Northerner after attending the last of two Funerals from the same Homestead"—a family that lost two sons, one a Confederate, the other a Union man. The Northerner likes certain aspects of Christianity no more than Melville does, scoring "the sanctioned sin of blood, / And Christian wars of natural brotherhood" ("A Meditation," 243). Against this, he acknowledges, as Ishmael would, "a darker side" to nature but also "Nature's charity," which rejects both the rebelliousness of the slaveholding South and the Pharisee self-righteousness of the abolitionist North. After all, Melville later writes in his own voice, the North might have seceded had the South been the stronger. "By how much more they boldly warred: / By so much more is mercy due" (ibid., 243). Or, as Melville puts it in his prose Supplement to the book, "Noble was the gesture into which patriotic passion surprised the people in a utilitarian time and country; yet the glory of the war falls short of its pathos—a pathos which now at least ought to disarm all animosity." "Benevolence and policy—Christianity and Machiavelli—dissuade from penal severities toward the subdued" ("Supplement," 265).

What of the freedmen? They deserve "the sympathies of every humane mind" in "their infant pupilage in freedom," which for now will mean "paternal guardianship" by the Reconstruction government. But care for the former slaves must not override "kindliness to communities who stand nearer to us in nature." By "nature" Melville may well mean 'racial' nature ("our white countrymen"); he might also mean nature in the sense of readiness for self-government. "For the future of the freed slaves we may well be concerned; but the future of the whole country, involving the future of the blacks, urges a paramount claim upon our anxiety" ("Supplement," 267). Southern whites are now surrounded by "millions of ignorant manumitted slaves," some of whom "now claim the suffrage." Are the ex-slaves ready for citizenship, or has slavery left too deep a mark on this generation of African-Americans? As Lincoln had argued before the war, the preservation of the Union is paramount to the settlement of the 'race question.' "Let us be Christians toward our fellow-whites, as well as philanthropists toward the blacks, our fellow-men [...]. Something may well be left to the graduated care of future legislation, and to heaven." Since "our institutions have a potent digestion," the American regime "may in time convert and assimilate to good all elements thrown in, however originally alien." Because the North won, vindicating the Union, Northerners are the ones who must now show "forbearance" ("Supplement," 268).

It has proven easy to attack Melville's appeal to 'white' racial affinities, but to do so ignores his desperation—seeing, as he does, with Lincoln (and the Founders), the importance of political union to the continued viability of republican self-government in the service of natural rights *for anyone*, of any 'race,' not only in the nineteenth century but in the twentieth and twenty-first centuries as well. The more urgent problem for Melville and other Americans of his generation was how to locate the Aristotelian 'mean' or 'middle' as reunion occurred. General Lee's speech to Congress is eloquent, but it is Melville's speech put into the mouth of Lee, not Lee's speech of that day. And even in Melville's poem, Lee speaks to Northern Republicans, not to 'his own' people. There was no Southern Grant, much less a Southern Lincoln—or if there was, he perished in the war, an outstretched hand to be clasped only in death.

Or was there a Southern Lincoln, who could not find a political place to stand in the postwar South? As for Lincoln himself, not only was he murdered, but he was not all mercy, even in victory. *Christian* charity or agape has its stern side, and Lincoln didn't intend to forgive all Southerners. He would have sent the leaders of secessionism into exile, even as the American Tories had been driven out, into Canada and elsewhere in the British Empire, after the Revolutionary War. Gradualism, yes: At the level of civil society, unjust prejudices can only die a slow death. But on the level of those potently digestive ruling institutions, the form or framework of the antebellum Southern state regimes, the aristocracy/oligarchy needed to go. On that, Thaddeus Stevens and the Radical Republicans were right, although in practice they failed, in part because they were insufficiently Lincolnian, unwilling or unable to exile the oligarchs. The result of a policy halfway between regime change and amelioration was a century of racial apartheid from which the country has yet fully to recover. Had oligarchs been exiled, could the voice of the minority Southern Whigs have been raised? Could there have been a Lincoln among them? It seems quite unlikely, but unknowable. Melville tells his readers to "revere that sacred uncertainty which forever impends over men and nations" ("Supplement," 268). He may not have revered it, exactly, in the privacy of his own mind, nor considered it sacred, but he did respect it as more powerful than manmade 'idealisms.'

There was no Southern Melville, either, at least not until Faulkner. In Melville's time, the South had its great comic counterpart to the tragedian of the North. Mark Twain attempted to teach in comedy some of what Melville taught in tragedy. Comedy works best in civil society, and thus gradually. For more immediate political purposes, Melville could never address the South the way he could address the North, but Southerners too needed his lesson in moderation, as the war proved an imprecise teacher.